Nick Vandome

100 TOP TIPS

Stay Safe Online and Protect Your Privacy

in easy steps

In easy steps is an imprint of In Easy Steps Limited
16 Hamilton Terrace · Holly Walk · Leamington Spa
Warwickshire · United Kingdom · CV32 4LY
www.ineasysteps.com

Notice of Liability
Every effort has been made to ensure that this book contains accurate and
current information. However, In Easy Steps Limited and the author shall
not be liable for any loss or damage suffered by readers as a result of any
information contained herein.

Trademarks
All trademarks are acknowledged as belonging to their respective
companies.

In Easy Steps Limited supports The Forest Stewardship Council (FSC), the
leading international forest certification organization. All our titles that are
printed on Greenpeace approved FSC certified paper carry the FSC logo.

MIX
Paper from
responsible sources
FSC® C020837

Printed and bound in the United Kingdom

ISBN 978-1-84078-867-9

Contents

100 TOP TIPS

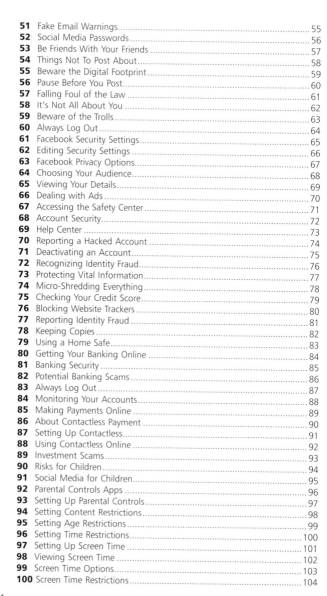

About Online Security

Online security is, or should be, the most important issue for anyone using a device that has online access; i.e., connects to the internet and the vast array of options that are available on it. From email to instant messaging, web pages to social media apps, there is not a corner of the internet that is not affected by security issues.

Online security threats come from an extensive range of sources. At times, the range and volume of potential threats can seem rather bewildering and overwhelming. However, being aware of the threats is the first step to being able to nullify them. Some of the potential security threats include:

- **Hackers**. These come in a variety of forms and are generally involved in creating malicious computer programs to harm computers and mobile devices.

- **Phishers**. A form of hacking, this involves trying to gain people's sensitive data and then exploit it.

- **Password vulnerability**. Weak or ineffective passwords can be the first way in which hackers can gain access to your devices.

- **Router vulnerability**. If your home internet router is not secure, this could be the first channel for people to gain access to your online systems and information.

- **Online scams**. These take numerous forms, from email scams offering large sums of money to fake advertising on social media sites.

- **Identity fraud**. This involves criminals gathering as much information as possible about someone and then pretending to be them, for financial gain.

- **Trolls**. An increasingly common aspect of social media, this involves spreading malicious comments and statements about other people.

Although online security is of paramount importance for all users of the internet, physical security should not be overlooked either. In some cases, physical security lapses can be the first step to opening the door to attacks on your online systems. Some areas of physical security to consider in relation to staying safe online:

- Never write down passwords for your devices and websites. If you have to do this, keep them in a secure location and do not keep them with the devices themselves.

- Keep all of your devices locked with passwords, so other people cannot use them and then access your personal data because they are not locked.

- Shred any sensitive documents with a micro-shredder (see Tip 74). This should ensure that the documents cannot then be reconstituted by someone else.

- Do not throw away any sensitive documents into the trash, as anyone could then access them and potentially commit identify theft.

- Check your online bank accounts regularly to ensure that there are not any suspicious transactions that you do not recognize. If there are, contact your bank immediately.

- Check your credit score with one of the online credit checking websites. If your score unexpectedly goes down, this could be a sign of some unauthorized activity as a result of identity fraud.

- Make sure that any old computing equipment – including desktop computers, laptops and tablets – is completely destroyed, or better still, disposed of by a professional company. Ensure that all of the data on the devices is wiped clean.

Securing Sensitive Data

Sensitive data on your computing devices is anything that you do not want someone else to see. It could be personal details that you do not want to be widely available, or financial details of online bank accounts. These details could be embarrassing or, worse, financially compromising. Even if the details themselves are not of interest to someone else, if they access your data and systems they may then be able to wreak havoc further afield and with other people; e.g., if they gain access to your online address book and contacts.

To ensure that your sensitive data is as secure as possible there are a few steps that can be taken:

● Use secure passwords on all of your digital devices, even if they are not connected to the internet: there could still be sensitive data on the device that could be accessed and used against you. Ensure that passwords are a minimum of eight characters (and preferably longer) and a mixture of uppercase and lowercase letters, numbers and symbols.

● Never divulge passwords to anyone, not even family members. If you tell someone else your password then your online security could be out of your own hands.

● Use anti-virus and firewall software. This is not foolproof, but it will help guard against a wide range of viruses and malicious software.

● Be careful when using public Wi-Fi hotspots. Do not access any of your own sensitive data when using a Wi-Fi hotspot, as it is possible for someone nearby to access your details through the hotspot.

● Never click on links in emails from people you don't know. Even if it is from someone that you do know, always be wary of links in emails, as the emails themselves could be fake ones from a hacker who has gained access to one of your friends' contacts lists.

Using Anti-Virus Software

Anti-virus software is one answer to the computer hackers, but it is fighting a never-ending battle, with the hackers frequently one step ahead and constantly developing new malicious programs.

Once anti-virus software is installed on your device it then scans your system looking for a catalog of viruses and related malicious software. When it finds a malicious item it will try to disable it and give you the chance to remove it. In some cases it will not be possible to remove the virus completely, in which case the anti-virus software will try to quarantine it instead, to limit its impact. Scans can be set to be performed automatically at specific times, or they can be performed manually at any time.

Some anti-virus software is free, while other options charge an annual or monthly fee. The reason for this is not only the initial cost of the software, but also for the updates they receive on a regular basis (usually at least once a day) to fight new viruses as they are released and identified.

At times it can seem a little inconvenient to run scans with anti-virus software, but it is a lot better than the alternative: your device becoming infected with viruses.

Anti-virus software will not always pick up every virus, particularly the most recently developed ones. Because of this it is a good idea to keep an eye on websites that report new viruses as they are discovered.

Only install and use one anti-virus product at a time. If you install two or more, they may try to compete with each other, causing inaccurate reporting and your computer to be less efficient and run slowly.

Firewalls are used to try to stop malicious software before it reaches your devices, by blocking it between your router and your devices. Firewall software frequently comes bundled with anti-virus packages, and the two programs can be used in tandem to fight against unwanted attacks.

Identifying New Viruses

Anti-virus software tries to keep as up-to-date as possible in terms of the latest viruses that are being developed. However, you can also keep an eye on this yourself.

- Follow technology news websites to get the latest news about the newest viruses and what impact they have.

- Look at the website of your anti-virus software provider for a range of news about new viruses and general information about dealing with viruses.

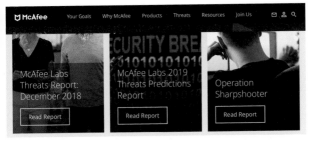

- Follow websites that are specifically aimed at identifying the latest viruses and online scams. Enter **latest computer viruses** as a web search phrase and explore the results.

Router Security

For the majority of homes with internet access the main method of communicating with these devices will be through your home Wi-Fi network. Therefore it is important that this network is as secure as possible. This starts with the Wi-Fi router, which is the device that connects your home devices to the internet wirelessly.

If your router has security weaknesses this means that hackers could be able to access your internet connection by gaining control of your router. This could be done remotely, so you would not know that it had happened. If hackers gain control of your router they would then be able to gain access to your devices and view your web activity; e.g., if you were undertaking online banking then they could acquire your login details, with all of the potential damage that could ensue.

There are some security areas that should be considered when using a router.

- **Firewall**. A Wi-Fi router that uses a recognized firewall should be used, as this will help to prevent malicious software and programs infecting your system.

- **Encryption**. This should be used by your router, to ensure that all communication is encrypted to make it much harder to be hacked or intercepted.

- **Auto-updating**. Routers sometimes have software updates that are designed to improve security or patch any flaws that have been identified. Look for a router that does this automatically whenever an update is available.

- **Change the default router password**. See Tip 7.

Check the specifications of the router before you buy it to see its security features.

Changing a Router Password

One area of security weakness for Wi-Fi routers can be their admin password. This is set when the router is manufactured and is generally very basic, along the lines of "admin" or "password". It is therefore important to change this password as soon as possible, to make it more secure. To do this:

1 Open a web browser and type the router's address in the address bar. (This is usually in the form of 192.168.1.1 or similar. Check with the documentation that came with the router, or search on the web using your router's model name)

2 Enter the **Username** and **Password**. If these have never been changed they should be along the lines of **Admin** and **Password**. Check the router's documentation if you are unsure about the default login details

Login

Enter your username and password to access your Technicolor Gateway.

Username: admin

Password: ●●●●●●●●●●●

(OK) (Cancel)

3 Access the section for changing the password, and update the router with a secure password

This page allows you to change your password based on your current one.

▸ **Change Password**

Old Password:

New Password:

Confirm New Password:

(Change Password) (Cancel)

Using Wi-Fi Hotspots

If you are away from home and your own Wi-Fi network, it is still possible to connect to the internet using public Wi-Fi connections, known as hotspots. These are Wi-Fi connections that are set up in public places such as cafes, libraries, and hotels, which can be used by anyone with the login name and password. In some instances, public hotspots do not require any login details and they are available to anyone who is within range of the hotspot router.

Although public hotspots are very convenient for accessing the internet when you are not at home, the main issue is that they are not as secure as using your home network. This is because it is easier for someone else to gain access to the Wi-Fi hotspot and, if they have the required skills, then view the details of whatever you are looking at on your device that is also connected to the hotspot.

Because of the security issues related to Wi-Fi hotspots there are some activities that you should be very careful with when using them:

- **Use of passwords and login details**. Hackers could be able to retrieve these if you were entering them at a Wi-Fi hotspot.

- **Online banking details** (either through a web browser or a banking app). It could be possible for hackers to steal these details through the public hotspot.

- **Use of debit or credit cards for online payments**. If you are making payments in this way, hackers could gain details of your cards and then make payments on your accounts.

If the hotspot requires a password to connect to it, this makes it slightly more secure, but not much. In most instances, hotspots should be safe to use, but if in doubt, do not enter any personal details into your device when you are using a public Wi-Fi hotspot.

Disposing of Old Devices

In the fast-moving world of technology, hardware devices become obsolete reasonably quickly, or people simply want to upgrade to the latest device. There are several options for disposing of old devices, but be aware of the security issues:

- **Sell them**. Online auction sites such as eBay are ideal for selling old PCs, laptops, tablets, and smartphones. Make sure you post an accurate description of the device and ensure that it is in good working order.

- **Trade them in**. A number of websites will quote you a trade-in price for your device.

- **Recycle them**. Numerous companies will recycle old computing devices, and some manufacturers will also take back their own old devices and recycle them.

- **Give them to family and friends**.

- **Donate them to charity**. Several charity organizations make good use of old computing equipment.

Whatever you do with your old devices, it is essential that you have wiped all of the data from them. There are a few ways in which to do this:

- Use software that is specifically designed to wipe data from computing devices.

- Go to a computing service that specializes in deleting data from devices.

- For smartphones and tablets, reset them to their factory setting, which erases the data on them. This option is usually found in the device's Settings app.

- Adopt the manual approach and destroy the device, using strong nails and a hammer.

When it's not Good to Share

In the online world, sharing photos, documents, and files is a way of life. It is becoming increasingly easy to do this, using a variety of methods including email, messaging, social media, and cloud services. However, as far as online security is concerned there are a number of areas where it is definitely not good to share information. Some of these are:

- **Usernames**. These frequently involve an email address, which in itself cannot really be kept secret. However, if a username is specifically created for a website or an app, it should not be disclosed.

- **Passwords**. These are the most important elements in the security of your online accounts and should never be shared with anyone.

- **Any security questions**. These are sometimes used to verify login information, and you can usually choose these questions when you create an online account for something.

Due to the amount of valuable information that can be obtained with login details there is no shortage of ways in which criminals try to get people to share these details. In all of these instances you should never share any passwords or login details.

- **Requests via email**. These often claim that an account has been locked and can only be unlocked by clicking on a link. But never click on any links in emails.

- **Requests from your bank**. Fake emails pretending to be from banks are used to try to obtain details for online bank accounts.

- **Requests via text messages**. These are used in a similar way to emails to try to get people to send them their login details for online accounts.

Always be Suspicious

A useful maxim to follow in life is, "If it seems too good to be true, then it probably is". The same can be said about a range of online offers and special deals. It is a good policy to always be slightly cynical and suspicious about any online activity that doesn't feel quite right. There are numerous ways in which hoaxers and fraudsters will try to take advantage of people online, and some to look out for include:

- **Email offers**. The concept of get-rich-quick schemes from foreign princes is now a well-known one on the internet. However, it is still in existence and people are still falling foul of it. Basically, it involves an email saying that there is a large sum of money awaiting the recipient, if they send a small admin fee to unlock the funds. Of course the money does not exist and the admin fee is never seen again.

- **Pensions offers**. Unsolicited offers to increase your pension, or release some equity from your pension, should always be treated with a large pinch of salt. Consult an accountant or an independent financial advisor before making any decision about your pension.

- **Share offers**. Get-rich-quick share offers also proliferate on the web. Known as "boiler-room scams", they promote shares in companies that offer incredible returns. Even if the companies are real, the returns invariably are not.

- **Hidden charges for items on social media sites**. This could look like a harmless survey, or free game, but there can be charges that are added to your cell/mobile phone bill or hidden subscriptions to paid-for services.

If you are ever tempted by an online offer, but you are not completely sure about it, check the details using an internet search engine to see if other people have come across it and what their experience of it has been. Also, take some time to think about it properly before you commit yourself financially to anything.

Avoiding Online Dangers

Given the number of potential online dangers it is perhaps surprising that so many of us commit so many aspects of our lives to the online world. Some issues to consider are:

- Never reply to any online communication from someone you do not know. This includes in email, text messages, and social media. It is easy to pretend to be someone that you are not when you have the anonymity of online communication. If in doubt about something, do not reply to it.

- Never open attachments in emails from unknown sources. This is because they could contain viruses that may then infect your computer, smartphone, or tablet. Even if you receive an unusual attachment from a trusted source it can be worth double-checking with them to ensure that it is has been checked for viruses.

- When possible, use virus software and a firewall. This can check your device for malicious software, try to block unwanted items before they reach your device, and scan attachments to ensure that they are virus-free.

- Never reply to online requests immediately. Whatever the request, always take a bit of time to think it over and, if possible, do some background checking on the person or organization making the request. Perform a search on the internet using their details to see if anything untoward is reported.

- Go for the nuclear option and disconnect a device from the internet, known as "air gapping" the device. This may seem rather drastic, as it will cut you off from the wealth of opportunities on the internet. However, if you use a specific computer solely for one purpose, such as work, it could be worth disabling internet access on this device so that it will be protected against any new online threats. Other digital devices could then be used for any internet access that is required.

Don't Leave it Unprotected

Passwords are the first line of defense against someone trying to gain unauthorized access to your personal data. However, it is worrying how often people do not add a password to their digital devices. This is not always helped by the portrayal of IT issues in movies and TV shows: frequently in thrillers or detective shows, the hero wanders over to a colleague's PC to gather a vital piece of evidence, or a smartphone is recovered and, miraculously, access is immediately achieved. This should never happen in real life! Every digital device that you use, from a home laptop, to a desktop PC at work, to your smartphone and tablet, should have a password assigned to it. Once this has been done, make sure that you lock your device whenever you are not using it; once it is locked it will require the password to unlock it and make it available for use.

If you do not have a password assigned to one of your devices it could have serious consequences. For your own personal devices this could be revealing your personal and private details to anyone who has access to your smartphone or tablet. However, in a work environment it could have more serious consequences: most organizations have a policy that individuals are responsible for the information on the computers that they use. If you do not protect your device with a password, or leave it unlocked when you are away from your computer, then you will be responsible for any unauthorized activity that is performed on your computer. In some cases this can result in serious disciplinary measures, including termination of employment.

Another consequence of leaving devices unprotected, or unlocked, is that it can be one of the first steps for hackers or fraudsters gaining access to your sensitive online details, such as those for online banking. If someone can access your computer, tablet, or smartphone through the lack of a password, it will give them the opportunity to access items such as your banking apps and attempt to perform fraudulent activity within them. Before you start using any digital device, assign a Lock screen password to it.

Creating a Strong Password

Passwords are not the most exciting aspect of the online world, but they are one of the most important. The emphasis is not just about using passwords, but creating strong passwords that are difficult for hackers or fraudsters to guess. Some areas to consider for strong passwords are:

- Make passwords a minimum of eight characters long, preferably more.

- Use a combination of uppercase and lowercase letters, numbers, and symbols.

- Don't use obvious words or combinations, such as family names, pets' names, sports teams, and birth dates. It may be hard to believe, but two of the most common passwords are PASSWORD and 123456. Never presume that hackers won't try the simplest passwords.

- Pick words at random; e.g., from a book or magazine and combine two words. But don't just use the words as they are: change the letters around and don't use single words as a password.

- Use a different password for different online accounts. If one is hacked, other accounts should still be secure.

- Try to change your passwords regularly, in case hackers manage to compromise them. Some systems in the workplace automatically ask you to change your password after a certain time period of using the same one, usually approximately every 90 days. For personal use this is more up to the individual: it can be irritating changing all of your passwords every three months or so, and it also means that you have a collection of new passwords to remember. Sometimes, if there is a security issue with an online service or website, you may be asked to change your password before you can access your account again. If this happens, check that it is a legitimate request, rather than a scam email.

Password Security

It make little sense to create a strong password, only to then make it readily available to people either deliberately or inadvertently. Some issues to consider are:

- Don't store a record of your passwords online (unless you're using a password manager – see Tip 17) – if a hacker gets into this then they have easy access to all of your accounts.

- Never share a password with anyone, even family members. Once a password has been shared it could easily be distributed to a wider audience and fall into the hands of hackers. It may seem harmless at the time, but if your password gets into the public domain due to your own actions, you will be responsible for all of the consequences that follow.

- Never click on a link in an email that asks for your password to restore an online account that has been blocked. This could be for an online bank account, or a social media account. Scam emails like this are increasingly common and should never be replied to. A reputable organization should never ask for your password in this way.

- If you need to write down your passwords, store them away from your computer in a secure location such as a home safe. This may seem like an unnecessary precaution, but passwords stored in desk drawers or under mouse mats are easy prey for anyone trying to gain unauthorized access to your devices, and you may be responsible if your devices are accessed due to your own lack of security precautions. Although it seems improbable that major companies would not have robust IT security protocols in place, there has even been a case where a manager proudly announced to an IT auditor that he never forgot his passwords for multiple accounts, because he had them all written down on a whiteboard in his office!

Also known as multi-factor authentication, two-factor authentication (2FA) is a security feature that requires a user logging in to an account on a website or an app to present two pieces of unique information in order to gain access to the account. One piece of information is the combination of username and password. The second piece of information is something that is generated at random once the first piece of information has been entered correctly.

Two-factor authentication is frequently used in conjunction with smartphones: when the user wants to log in to an account, a one-time passcode is generated once they have entered their username and password. This is sent to their smartphone and once the passcode has been entered successfully, the user will have access to their online account.

If an online account supports two-factor authentication you will be asked if you want to use this when you log in to the account. A smartphone number will need to be linked to the account, so that the one-time passcode can be sent to it. If an account has two-factor authentication, then it should be used, to make the account much more secure.

When you log in to a two-factor authentication account, a passcode field will appear. The passcode will be sent to your smartphone and can be entered from here.

About Password Managers

One way to create strong passwords automatically is to use a password manager. This is an app that performs a number of security options relating to secure passwords. All you need to do is remember one password, for your password manager (this makes it even more important to ensure that your password for the password manager is stored securely).

Password managers can be downloaded from app stores connected to desktop PCs or laptops, and also the app stores connected to smartphones and tablets. If you use a password manager, ensure that it is downloaded to all of your digital devices, so that if a strong password is

automatically generated on one device, it will be recognized by the password manager on all of your other devices. Some of the features of a password manager to look for are:

- **Password generator**. This is used by the manager to create very complex and secure passwords, which it duly remembers for you.

- **Encryption**. Make sure that the password manager encrypts your passwords and saves them securely, so that even if the password manager site was hacked, your passwords will be safely encrypted.

- **Cross-device compatibility**. Some password managers are specific to a single operating system; e.g., iOS on the iPhone or iPad. Others can be used across devices using different operating systems.

- **In-app purchases**. A lot of password managers are free to download, but have a paid-for version that can involve an annual subscription. This does not have to be used, but it does add extra functionality.

When you first open a password manager app that you have downloaded, you will be asked to create an account with the app. This involves creating a master password that will be known only to you. As shown in Tip 14, ensure that the password is as strong as possible. The app will usually have a minimum level of strength required for logging in.

Once you have logged in to a password manager you can explore its features. These should include the tools for managing passwords. They can be used to create new strong passwords and also create online passwords for websites, using their own browser option.

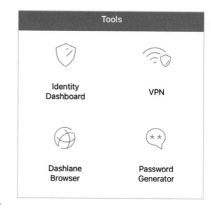

Generating Passwords

The password generator within a password manager app is an excellent option for creating passwords that can be stored securely within the app. Once this has been done they can be entered manually on a website or within an app, or the password manager can auto-fill the details as required. To generate passwords within a password manager:

1 Open the **Password Generator**

2 A strong password will have already been created

3 Make the required selections for the criteria for the strong password; e.g., a longer minimum length

< Tools	Password Generator

jN$C;s[g10'^

Refresh

Copy

LENGTH: 12

4 ————————————— 40

OPTIONS

Digits

Letters

Symbols

4 Tap on the **Copy** button to save the password within the password manager (see Tip 20). Tap on the **Refresh** button to generate a new strong password

Once a password has been generated and copied within a password manager, it can then be assigned to a website for creating an online account as part of the login details for the account. When the account is created, use the strong password that has been created by the password manager. To do this:

 Copy the password as shown in Tip 19. Tap on the **Save** option

> Your password has been copied. Do you want to save it in Dashlane?
>
> Save

 Enter the name of the website to be used, a username, and the website address. The password will already be added. Tap on the eye icon next to the password to view it. Tap on the **Save** button to save these details in the password manager. When a new account is created for the specified website, the password can be copied from the password manager and used on the site. This will then be remembered the next time you want to log in to your account on this site

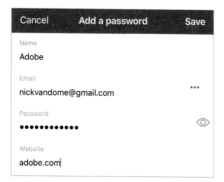

Changing Passwords

Changing passwords regularly (every three months or so) is good IT practice, and in some working environments it is compulsory (after a period of time the system will prompt you to create a new password). Rather than merely adding an extra number to the end of an existing password, a password manager can be used to create and store a new password every time that you need to change it. The new password will then be stored in the password manager, and you can check it here if you forget it. To do this:

Save a password as shown in Tip 20. Instead of adding website details, give the password a name related to your work and leave the website address blank. The email address should be the same as the one you use to log in to your work system. Tap on the **Save** button

Cancel	Add a password	Save

Name
My Office

Email
nickvandome@gmail.com   •••

Password
•••••••••••• 👁

Website
www.example.com

Tap on the eye icon to view the password and enter it as your work login. Repeat this whenever you need to change a password

Password
55_jSndBY|W+ 👁

Using Passwords in Public

There are enough potential dangers when using passwords in the relative safety of your own home. These are usually connected to virtual threats. However, once you are out in public, a whole new range of potential problems arise. Some of the virtual ones remain, but physical ones also come into play once you are in public. Some issues to consider are:

- **People viewing your passwords**. When traveling on public transport you should be very wary about entering passwords into your devices. It is easy for people beside you or behind you to see the details that you are entering. If someone has malicious intent, they could memorize your password and then try to get their hands on your device. This not only compromises your online security, but it could put your personal safety at risk if someone tries to physically take your device once they have learnt your password.

- **Reflected passwords**. Even if someone is not sitting near to you in public this does not mean that they cannot still try to see your password if you are entering it into your device. Reflections in windows on public transport can be used to see what is being entered into a smartphone or tablet. If you do have to enter a password in public, try to keep it hidden by using your hand to shield the keypad as you are entering it. Even better, use finger identification or face recognition as your password, rather than having to physically enter details on a keypad (see Tips 23 and 24).

- **Harvesting passwords from public Wi-Fi hotspots**. By their nature, public Wi-Fi hotspots offer access to anyone within range of the Wi-Fi router, usually with a password that is available from the establishment offering the service. This makes hotspots a greater security risk than a home router that can have a private password applied to it. Hackers can use hotspots to gain access to other users of the hotspot and mirror any of their activities, such as entering passwords.

Your Finger is Your Password **23**

Smartphones and tablets increasingly use fingerprint recognition as the password for unlocking a device. Since every fingerprint is unique it is more secure than a user-generated password. However, a physical password is still required to be added to the device, in case the fingerprint recognition does not work. If a device supports fingerprint recognition as a password it is usually set up in the Settings app. The general process to do this is:

 Open the Settings app and access the **Touch ID** option. Create a passcode, which is required if the fingerprint sensor does not work for any reason

2 Tap on the **Add a Fingerprint...** option. This presents a screen for creating your Touch ID

FINGERPRINTS

Finger 1 〉

Add a Fingerprint...

 Place your finger on the Home button several times until the Touch ID is created. This will include capturing the edges of your finger. The screens move automatically after each part is captured, and the

Cancel

Place Your Finger

Lift and rest your finger on the Home button repeatedly.

fingerprint icon turns red. Once this is completed you will be able to use your fingerprint to unlock your device

27

A similar option to unlocking devices with fingerprint identification is using face recognition. This uses a sophisticated combination of sensors and cameras on a smartphone or tablet to unlock the device simply by looking at the screen. The systems are very accurate and it means that your device can only be unlocked by you looking at it. Face recognition can also be used for a range of other options that traditionally require a password, such as contactless payment and online payment on websites that support face recognition. As with fingerprint identification, face recognition also requires a password as backup, in case it does not work for any reason. To set up face recognition on a compatible device:

Open the Settings app and access the **Face ID** option. Create a passcode, which is required if face recognition does not work for any reason

2 Position your face in the center of the circle that accessed the device's camera. Move your head slowly in a circle so that the camera can record all of your facial features (face recognition can accurately recognize faces, even if the user is wearing glasses or a hat)

Tap on the **Done** button to finish the Face ID setup process

Resetting a Password

If you think that one of your online passwords has been compromised, it is possible to reset it from the login screen for related websites or apps. For some sites this is more straightforward than others: if you want to reset a password for online banking, or other sites that involve financial transactions, the process may require a new password to be sent to you through the post, rather just changing it online. However, in most cases it can be done by clicking on a link on the website or in the app. This can also be done for forgotten passwords, or just because you want to change it.

 Access the login page for the site or app whose password you want to reset. Select the **Forgot password?** (or Reset password) option

> **Log in**
>
> Forgot password? · Sign up for Twitter

 Enter the email address that is linked to the account (usually the username). An email will be sent to this address, containing details about how to reset the password

🐦 Password Reset   English ▾

How do you want to reset your password?

We found the following information associated with your account.

🔘 Email a link to **ni********@m**.*****

Continue

Don't Go Phishing

Online hackers and fraudsters are very innovative, and they are constantly looking for new ways to gain people's personal information. One of the most common of these is phishing. Phishing is the act of trying to get people to divulge personal details of online accounts, such as usernames, passwords, and financial details. Once the fraudsters have these details they can attempt to access your accounts by pretending to be you. The more information that they have, the easier it can be for them. Phishers generally operate by sending a bogus email stating that there is a problem with a certain type of account, and asking you to click on a link in the email to fix the problem. These types of emails could include the following:

- A message from a cloud service, such as iCloud or Google Drive, saying that your account has been locked. The email requests that you click on the link to unlock the account.

- A message from on online retailer saying that your account has been suspended due to irregular activity on your account. These usually appear to originate from the large, well-known online retailers, thus increasing the chances that the recipient really does have an account with them, to make the phishing email seem more believable.

- A message from a bank saying that your online account has been suspended.

- A message from a courier service saying that there is a problem with a delivery that they have for you.

Regardless of how plausible a phishing email may seem, do not click on the link in the email, as this is the first step to giving the fraudsters your personal information. There are some measures that can be taken to identify phishing emails and these are looked at in Tips 48 and 49.

Viruses can be Sickening

There is a range of malicious software (malware) that can infect your computing devices and compromise them in various ways. One of the original ones is the virus. This is a malicious software program that installs itself on the victim's computer without their knowledge. When it is activated (frequently this is done automatically by the code within the virus) the virus then conducts its malicious mission. This can cause a range of problems, including:

- The operating system fails to start, or takes repeated attempts to boot up.

- All files of a certain type are deleted; e.g., all photos or word processing files.

- Folders within your file system disappearing without explanation.

- All contacts in an address book are sent random emails. You may only realize this if they contact you and ask about a strange email that they have received from you. Similarly, if you receive a strange email from one of your contacts it could mean that their computer has been infected with a virus. The email could also contain the virus within it, so don't open any attachments.

- Error messages that appear frequently and with no explanation.

- Slow performance and frequent crashes and freezes.

- Any erratic or unexplained behavior that starts happening regularly could be an indication that your device has a virus.

Viruses usually get into devices through clicking on an infected attachment in an email or a link to a website containing the virus. If in doubt, don't click on links in emails from sources that you don't know.

Operating systems that run desktop computers, laptops, tablets and smartphones are not exempt from viruses and some hackers specifically target operating systems such as Windows 10, macOS, iOS and Android. Because of this, operating systems frequently have security updates that are aimed at preventing any virus threats that have been identified. They can also be used to fix any security flaws that have been identified within the operating system.

Because of the importance of the operating system to a computing device (without it, the device would be rendered useless) it is vital that security updates are installed as soon as they are released. There are two ways to do this (both options are usually accessed from the device's Settings app):

● Select for updates to be installed automatically.

● Select manual updates, which involves checking for available updates and then deciding whether to install them or not.

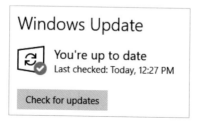

Worming Their Way In

A worm is a type of virus that can perform a number of disruptive tasks on an infected machine. Worms can attach themselves to a device through an attachment in an email, a link to a site hosting the worm, or through security vulnerabilities within a device's operating system.

Once a worm has found a host computer it can replicate itself automatically from computer to computer over the internet. As with other viruses, worms can perform a range of destructive tasks:

- Modifying or deleting files, without the knowledge of the computer's user.

- Deploying additional malicious software within the device. This can be designed to perform a specific task.

- Disrupting a system simply by replicating itself multiple times. This has the effect of overloading the system, leading to a major deterioration in performance.

- Replicating itself via email by using the user's address book to send itself to all of the contacts. As with viruses, a strange email from one of your contacts could be a sign that they have a worm – if it doesn't look right, don't click on anything in the email, and contact the sender.

Some of the signs that your device may have a worm are:

- The available storage space on your computer's hard drive can be drastically reduced, as the worm replicates itself within your operating system.

- Devices run slowly and take longer than normal to perform specific tasks.

- Files are mysteriously deleted, or additional ones appear in your file management system.

Named after the Wooden Horse of Troy from Greek mythology, modern-day computer Trojans perform an equally devious and destructive operation as their Greek namesake. The original Wooden Horse of Troy was presented as an innocent gift, but housed armed troops who revealed themselves and wreaked havoc once the Wooden Horse was safely inside their enemies' city walls.

A modern computer Trojan is a seemingly innocent piece of software (such as a game or a utility program) that contains a malicious payload within it, tricking the user into opening it in an updated version of the Greek Wooden Horse of Troy. When the software is opened or activated, the Trojan is released. Trojans usually have several malicious functions including gathering information from your device, as well as performing destructive tasks.

One way in which Trojans gain information from an infected device is known as "keylogging", whereby the Trojan copies all of the keystrokes used by the user, thus being able to find out usernames and passwords when these are entered on websites or within apps. Keylogging can also be used to obtain your debit or credit card details by copying your keystrokes if you are buying anything online.

Another function of Trojans is to generate false adverts that appear as pop-up messages on an infected device. These claim that your device has been infected by a virus, and that you need to download the advertised anti-virus software to resolve the issue. The anti-virus software does not exist, and the advertisement only serves to harvest the user's credit card details if they attempt to buy it.

Trojans are frequently hidden in innocent-looking apps such as games. In general, apps from recognized app stores are subject to more checks than those from third-party sites. However, this does not mean that they are immune from Trojans, but it is better to download apps from a recognized store, such as the default one linked to your device.

Holding You To Ransom

While a lot of malicious software performs its destructive tasks in the background, there is one form of malware that will stop you in your tracks if it infects your device: ransomware. This is a particularly devious form of malicious software that creates a pop-up message detailing a range of security threats that have befallen your device, and demanding payment to solve the issue, usually by credit card or a cryptocurrency such as Bitcoin. There are several types of ransomware, but payment should never be made as a result of them. If it does happen, consult a computing security professional.

- **Stand-alone pop-up messages**. These are designed more to panic the user into making a payment. The message may say that malicious software has been detected on their device and it can be removed by following the payment details in the pop-up message. If you can still access your files, and your device is working normally, then the message can probably be ignored.

- **Locked screens**. A more serious issue is if the ransomware infects your device so that you are locked out of it and cannot access any files. This will be accompanied by an official-looking message detailing how to unlock your device by making a payment.

- **Encrypted files**. This is the most serious form of ransomware: all of your files are encrypted so that they cannot be accessed. A pop-up message offers, for a fee, a key to decrypt the files. For some ransomware the key does not exist, even if payment is made.

One important issue in relation to ransomware is to ensure that all of your files are backed up regularly: if the worst does happen then at least you will not have lost all of your files and documents. Although individuals are targeted with ransomware, it is more common for it to be directed at large organizations, when the cyber criminals demand a fee for each device that is encrypted.

Even if you do not have any viruses on your computer or mobile devices this does not mean that you are immune from malicious software. We are all becoming increasingly dependent on the online world, which means that if there is a disruption to this it can have a negative impact on our daily lives. This may be something non-essential such as not being able to log in to a social media site, but there are also some more serious consequences if you rely on online financial services or online tickets for an event or journey. (If you do rely on online tickets for something, it is worthwhile printing them out too, in case the online version is not available.) Attacks of this nature are known as Denial of Service (DoS) attacks, and are frequently aimed at large and high-profile websites in order to achieve recognition, or notoriety, for the hackers.

DoS attacks generally operate by bombarding an organization's computers with huge numbers of requests for authentication to access their website. This is a normal process, but DoS attacks do not have a valid internet address for the response from the target's servers. This means that the servers can become overwhelmed by authentication requests that they cannot meet, and this results in the servers being unable to perform their usual task of displaying an organization's website.

A DoS attack generally results in a website being unavailable, but it can also cause an ineffective or intermittent service from an affected website.

If you cannot access one of your regular websites it could mean it has fallen prey to a DoS attack. These are usually well documented within the media, but there may be a period of time until it is reported. Search for "service status" on the internet to see it there are any details of a DoS for the website that you are trying to access. It is unusual for a DoS attack to endure for more than a few hours, but it can be frustrating if you are trying to access a website that is under attack during this time.

Fake News

Although fake news has not been invented by the internet, in terms of its ability to reach huge audiences around the world at great speed, it is very much a product of the online age, and in particular social media. For news items, because it has been "published" on the internet it seems to gain more validity than something gossiped about over the water cooler. There are numerous issues related to fake news:

- Accept that fake news exists. One aspect of fake news is attempts to deny that certain things exist, or have happened. One of these is the existence of fake news itself: due to the easy way by which anyone can now publish what seems to be a genuine news item, the existence of fake news is undeniable.

- Social media should not be seen as a comprehensive alternative to traditional news outlets (although they may not always be completely accurate either).

- Be particularly wary during major ongoing news events. Social media is rife with rumors if there is a major natural disaster or a significant incident. There may be some accuracies within this, but a lot of the details that users post are inaccurate, or deliberately designed to confuse or misdirect. Do not rely solely on information on social media at times of crisis.

- Always look to check details with other news sites. For any news story on social media, double-check it with more traditional news websites. Journalists should check their facts before publishing stories, but the same constraints do not apply to social media.

- Don't just follow people/organizations whose views you share on social media. It is easy to become very narrow-minded if we just communicate with people who support our own social and political views. This is known as an "echo chamber", and it is good to be exposed to different views and opinions.

Fake Advertisements

Another area that has become a rich vein for online fraudsters is fake advertisement. Social media sites in particular are awash with advertising, with some of it being more genuine than others. Some areas where you can get caught out by fake advertisements include:

- Clickbait. These are advertisements or promotions that are simply designed to get users to click on a link that takes them to another website. They are frequently linked to stories about celebrities, to catch people's attention. The websites that are accessed from the original item may just be an attempt to promote another site, but they may have more serious consequences in terms of subscribing the user to certain services without their knowledge or approval.

- Products are simply not as they are portrayed, or do not exist. The role of advertising is to make items look as appealing as possible. However, with online advertisements it is easy to give a completely false description of something. Since a product cannot be physically seen or handled, the user is entirely at the mercy of the online description and photos of the product. Both of these can easily be faked and can lead to people sending money for something that is nothing like its description, or does not even exist at all.

- Advertisements that contain malicious software. One way in which hackers deploy viruses is through fake advertisement. When the user clicks on an item in the advertisement, it downloads the malicious software to their computer or mobile device.

When looking at any online advertisements, do an internet search about them before you have any interaction with the advertisement. If there is anything untoward about it then information about this will probably already be available somewhere on the internet.

Online and Phone Scams

There has been a huge range of cons and scams in operation well before the invention of the internet. However, the audience that can be reached in the online world, and the speed at which it can be done, means that this is a rich hunting ground for fraudsters. There are dozens of these scams that are perpetrated on the internet or via cell/mobile phones and some of them include:

- **Dating scams**. People on dating websites and apps befriend someone, enter into a relationship, and then ask for money from the other person.

- **Property scams**. Rental properties are particularly prone to scams where a property is advertised for rent, but it can only be viewed if a fee is paid upfront, never to be seen again.

- **Charity scams**. Fraudsters pretending to be organizing charity appeals occur on social media sites, harming both individuals and genuine charity appeals.

- **Prize scams**. These operate via an email or a text message that claims you have won a prize of some sort. However, a fee has to be paid to release the prize, or bank details are required for payment of the prize.

- **Tech support**. This involves a fraudster phoning and pretending to be technical support from a major computer company. Once they have the user's confidence, they extract a range of personal details.

- **Travel scams**. These involve fake websites that promote discounted travel tickets and offers. Only use travel sites that you know to be reputable.

A general rule with online or phone scams is: never engage with, or pay money to, anyone who sends you an unexpected or unsolicited email, social media request, text message, or phone message.

One of the most common ways for viruses and malicious software to enter a computing system is through files that are shared on peripheral devices such as flashdrives or CDs/DVDs. Files that are copied onto peripheral devices can contain viruses, either deliberately or inadvertently, and when they are opened on a computer, the virus infects the system.

Viruses can be transmitted via peripheral devices in a range of files, but particularly in games and utility apps used to perform tasks for maintaining a computer system. If you are given a peripheral device and it contains files or apps that you have not created or downloaded, it is important to check that there are no viruses within them. The best way to do this is to run a scan with anti-virus software. It should scan over your whole computer, including any peripheral devices that have been attached to external drives. However, sometimes this has to be specified within the settings of the anti-virus software: select any options that include external drives within the scan process.

In some cases, it is also possible to specifically ask for a scan over a peripheral device once it has been attached to an external drive. This is done by selecting the peripheral device in the computer's file management system and selecting a specific anti-virus option relating to the item in the external drive. Any adverse results will show up in the scan, or it will be reported as being virus-free (as far as the anti-virus software is concerned).

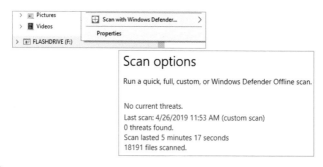

Getting Your Backup

One of the more tedious aspects of using computing devices is backing up the information on them. However, this is also a crucial task and one that should be included in any digital maintenance regime that you practice. If possible, every time you use a computer or a mobile device the data should be backed up afterwards. There are a number of ways in which backups for computers and mobile devices can be done:

- **Cloud backups**. This is done via the cloud storage service that is associated with the device. The files and documents on the device are backed up to an external computer, usually connected to the operating system of the device. The system files for the operating system can also be backed up in this way.

- **Hard drive backups**. This is done by attaching an external hard drive to the device (usually a desktop computer or a laptop) and copying files from the computer to the hard drive. If an external hard drive is used, store it away from the device itself.

- **Automatic backups**. Both cloud backups and external hard drive backups can be set to be performed automatically. This is the best option, as you do not have to remember to always manually back up files (although it can still be done manually). Automatic backups can be set to be performed at specific times, which is done within the settings of the device.

Backup

Back up using File History
Back up your files to another drive and resto
originals are lost, damaged, or deleted.

Automatically back up my files
⬤ On

⟨ iCloud   **Backup**

BACKUP

iCloud Backup   ⬤

Automatically back up data such as your accounts,
documents, Home configuration, and settings when this
iPhone is connected to power, locked, and on Wi-Fi. Learn
more...

Back Up Now

Looking for HTTPS

One of the great fears of using online websites that require the disclosure of financial details is that these will be misused, or accessed by hackers or fraudsters. This is a legitimate concern and companies invest considerable resources to ensure that their online transactions are as secure as possible.

There are two ways that users can initially check to see if a website that they are using is protected by security measures for financial transactions:

- **Look for HTTPS in the website address**. HTTP stands for Hypertext Transfer Protocol and this is the series of rules that are used for websites to communicate data with users. The important part of this is when the extra S is added. This stands for Secure, and indicates that a website uses encrypted security to ensure that information on the site is protected from attacks from anyone trying to intercept a communication between a user and the website. If you are using any kind of website that requires a financial transaction, look at the website address to ensure it starts with HTTPS.

- **Digital certification**. In addition to HTTPS, if a website has a padlock icon next to its address, this indicates that it is a secure connection. This digital certificate contains information that confirms that a website's connection is secure and that it provides a public key that enables the website and the user to communicate securely. The user is rarely aware of this, but if you click on the padlock icon you can view details about the digital certificate.

Creating fake websites is a method used by online fraudsters to try to steal people's money. A site is created that looks like a genuine retail or banking website, but when the users try to buy anything or enter their financial details, these are captured by the fraudsters. Efforts to detect fake websites can be done manually or automatically:

- Check to see if a site has HTTPS in its website address. If not, do not use it for financial transactions.

- Check to see if there is a padlock icon next to the website address, to ensure that communication with the site is secure.

- Check the full address of the website. Some fake websites generate website addresses that are displayed as a shortened version of the full name, and fraudsters can use this to display a plausible-sounding website. Click or tap in the address bar of the browser that you are using to display the full address for the web page that you are viewing.

- Look for obvious errors on the website, such as spelling or grammatical errors.

- Within the settings for the browser that is being used is often a function that can identify fraudulent websites, through their use, or lack of, a digital certificate. Turn this On to help your browser identify fake websites.

Fraudulent Website Warning	

Windows Defender SmartScreen
Help protect me from malicious sites and downloads with Windows Defender SmartScreen

On

Although they may not be the most exciting aspect of the online world, security and privacy settings for your devices are very important, and are your first line of defense against a range of potential threats aimed at your digital devices.

Different operating systems, and their related devices, have security settings that can be accessed in different ways:

- **Windows 10 PCs and laptops.** Security settings can be found in **Settings** > **Privacy** and also **Settings** > **Update & Security**.

- **Apple computers or laptops running macOS.** Security settings can be found in **System Preferences** > **Security & Privacy**.

- **iPhone and iPads running iOS.** Security settings can be found in **Settings** > **Privacy**.

- **Android smartphones and tablets** (depending on the device). Security settings can be found in **Settings** > **Privacy/Security**.

In addition to general security settings, website browsers also have a range of security options that can be applied when using that specific browser. This is more commonly available for browsers on desktop computers and laptops, rather than mobile devices.

>	**Privacy & security** ⊷
⚙ General	
🔒 Privacy & security	**Browsing data**
⚲ Passwords & autofill	Some features might save data on your device or send it to Microsoft to improve your browsing experience
⇵ Advanced	<u>Learn more about Microsoft privacy</u>
	Clear browsing data
	Includes cookies, history, passwords, and other data
	Choose what to clear

Applying Privacy Settings

Whether privacy and security settings occur within the settings section of a device, or within an individual app, each setting can be selected and either turned On or Off, or additional options can be accessed.

For some privacy and security settings, it is just a case of turning them On or Off.

For other settings, there is a range of options that apply to the main privacy and security item.

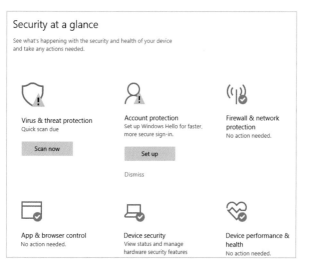

45

Cookies are small programs from websites that obtain details from your browser when you visit a site. The cookie remembers the details for the next time you visit the site. This can be useful for storing any information that you have entered into a website, such as form details or online shopping preferences. However, some people are wary of cookies and fear that they may gather data about their web browsing and pass it to a third party, without permission. This is a possibility, but there have been efforts in recent years to make the use of cookies more transparent. If a website is using cookies, it should display a message to this effect when you first visit the site, asking if you accept the use of cookies on your device. You can accept or decline them, and the message should only appear once.

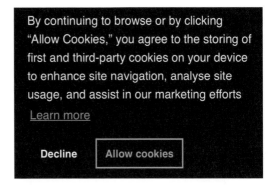

> By continuing to browse or by clicking "Allow Cookies," you agree to the storing of first and third-party cookies on your device to enhance site navigation, analyse site usage, and assist in our marketing efforts
>
> Learn more
>
> **Decline**   **Allow cookies**

Whether you accept cookies or not is a personal choice, but in general they are a benefit when browsing the web: try deleting all of the cookies and then see the items that you have to re-enter when you are browsing.

Cookies can be viewed (and deleted) in a browser's cache, usually accessible from the browser's privacy and security settings (see Tip 43). If you do elect to delete cookies, there will be a confirmatory message to double-check that this is what you want to do.

Clearing the Cache

A browser's cache is where website browsing history and related items are stored. It happens in the background so that you will not generally be aware of it. The cache remembers websites that you have visited, and this negates the need to reload websites when you return to them. (However, if new information has been added to the website since your last visit, you will need to refresh the page to show the latest information, rather than just the cached version that has been saved.)

Cached data can start to take up a certain amount of space in your browser, but it can be deleted to free up space or for any other reason why you may not want to store data that has accumulated while browsing the web. Depending on the type of device being used, there may be options to select what type of information you want to clear from the cache.

1 In the browser's privacy and security settings, select the option for clearing browsing data

> **Clear browsing data**
> Includes cookies, history, passwords, and other data
>
> Choose what to clear

2 Select the required items to be deleted

Filling in forms of any sort is one of life's chores, and it is no different in the online world. Forms are used for numerous purposes, particularly on the checkout page of online shopping websites. When you buy something from one of these sites, you need to enter your personal details, including name, address, and email address, as well as the details for the method of payment used. If you use an online shopping website regularly, it can become tiresome to enter the same details every time you make a purchase. The alternative is to use the auto-fill feature on the browser. If this is turned On, details that are entered into a form are remembered and automatically entered the next time that you want to fill in the form (when you click into one of the form fields you will be prompted to use auto-fill, if it has been activated).

Auto-fill is a very useful option, but it should not be activated if someone else has access to your computer, tablet, or smartphone; if they do, they may be able to make online purchases from your account, using auto-fill.

Auto-fill can be used to automatically enter your personal details, and also bank or credit card details that are used for purchases. These can be turned On or Off in the settings for the web browser being used. It is also possible to specify where your contact information is taken from.

‹ Safari	**AutoFill**	
Automatically fill out web forms using your contact or credit card info.		
Use Contact Info		⬤
My Info	Nick Vandome ›	
Credit Cards		⬤

Sending Money Online

Millions (if not billions) of financial transactions happen on the internet every day. It can be a quick and easy way to buy a variety of goods and services, and also send money to family and friends through online banking. Unfortunately, it is also a magnet for criminals and fraudsters. Because of the ease with which money can be sent online, it is important to follow a few simple rules:

- Never send money to someone who you do not know. If someone makes an unsolicited request for money, it is almost certainly fake.

- If you are unsure about a bank transfer, select a date in the future to make a payment rather than the Pay Now option. This will give you time to cancel the payment if you discover something untoward.

- Be wary of sending money to money transfer services. These are legitimate ways of sending money to people, particularly abroad, but fraudsters can also use them to ask for payment for something that is not delivered.

- Use a method of online payment that has some form of financial protection. Major credit cards are usually the best option for this.

- Check seller ratings on online auction sites. If someone has a history of not delivering items that have been paid for, then this will be flagged up very quickly.

- Users of travel websites in some geographic locations are protected for any loss incurred through the website (including a company going bankrupt, or a holiday being canceled).

- If in doubt about an online transaction, ask to use a third-party escrow service, which keeps the money in custody and only pays it out when certain terms agreed by the two parties involved have been met.

When conducting financial transactions with individuals on the internet, a good rule is to never trust someone's identity until you can verify it as fully as possible. On sites such as online auction sites, sellers usually have a list of feedback about their services, so any issues should be flagged up. However, for some transactions, particularly involving large sums of money, it can be harder to definitively check someone's identity. Some of the methods fraudsters use on online sites include:

- **Fake email addresses**. Since any name can be created for an email address, the name in the email may not bear any resemblance to the actual person.

- **Fake photos**. Some online sites contain profile photos of people selling goods or services. However, these are chosen by the seller, so a reassuring photo of a trustworthy-looking person could hide the true identity of a fraudster.

- **Financial requests**. Fraudulent online sellers will sometimes ask for some form of payment, such as a money transfer deposit, before an item is delivered. This should be resisted.

Ways in which someone's online identify can be checked are:

- Look at the email address. If it includes an actual name, this can be checked using other sources.

- Do an internet search for the person to see if anything comes up.

- Search social media to see if you can find the person, using their email address and profile photo.

- If possible, try to contact the person through another means except their given email address; e.g., directly through a telephone number that you have found.

Claims of Account Locking

Considering the number of online options that are available on the internet, it is understandable that people have an increasing number of online accounts; i.e., ones that are accessed with a login name and password. Online fraudsters try to take advantage of this by using fake emails that claim that an online account has been locked. These emails are sent under the guise of well-known popular websites, in the hope that the recipient of the email actually will have an account with the related website.

Emails containing claims of online accounts being locked look genuine enough (apart from the actual email address; see Tip 48).

If you do receive an email claiming that an account has been locked (and you have an account with the named service), the first thing to do is not to panic. Do not click on any links in the email. Instead, look up the actual website of the company and contact them via this to see if there are any genuine issues with your account.

Email addresses can be used to display anything in the From box when it is delivered to someone's Inbox. For instance, an email address of 123abc@gmail.com could display a completely different title in the From box: the display of an email address does not have to have any relation to the actual address. This means that online fraudsters can create emails that pertain to come from major companies, such as Facebook, Apple or USPS, while the actual email address is completely different. However, it is possible to see what the actual email address is:

 The textual title of an email can be displayed at the top of the email, in the **From** box

> From: United States Postal Service >
> To: ▓▓▓▓▓▓▓ Hide UP
>
> **Not possible to make delivery**
> April 14, 2019 at 00:11
>
> **⌥USPS.COM®**
>
> en-US
>
> **We have sent you a message**
>
> An email containing confidential personal information was sent to you
>
> **More information**
>
> **Sign in and get started!**
> http://www.usps.com/

 Tap or click on the title in the **From** box to display the actual email address. If it bears no resemblance to the company name then the email is probably a fake and should be deleted, without clicking on anything within it

Checking Email Content

In addition to checking the actual address of an email, it can also be possible to identify fake emails by the content of the email itself. Some items to look for include:

- Check the spelling within the email. If the email has originated from outside the country in which it is delivered, there may be spelling errors in the email. Look at the header items, such as the email title, as well as the body of the email.

- Check for grammar. Read the email carefully to see if there are any glaring grammatical errors.

- Check any company logos that are used in the email. In some cases, an old logo may have been used, so check on the company's own website to see if the logo and the associated tagline are the same.

- If you have undertaken a transaction with the company named in the email, check any reference numbers in the email with any online receipts you received when you first made the transaction. If in doubt, contact the company directly, through their website, but never through the fake email.

- If there is a **Click Here** website link, without the actual website address displayed, move the cursor over the Click Here text to display the actual website link and see if it bears any resemblance to the company name. In some cases, it may be similar to the company name but with subtle differences.

- If you have any concerns about an email that you have received, avoid clicking on any items within it and send it to the Junk folder within your emails. This means that similar emails should then begin to be sent to the Junk folder automatically (although this is not always the case if the fraudsters keep changing the email address associated with the email; see Tip 50).

Spam emails pretending to be from a recognized company can be hidden behind numerous different email addresses. For instance, similar-looking emails claiming that a certain online account has been locked can be sent with dozens of different hidden email addresses. This means that even if one email is sent to your Junk email folder, others could arrive in your Inbox because of the different email addresses. Even if you know that this is a fake email, it can become annoying having to send the messages to your Junk folder every time that they arrive. In this instance, two options should be avoided:

- Do not reply to the email to ask them to stop sending you messages.

- Do not use the **Unsubscribe** option to try to opt out of emails from this email address. This is an option that is usually displayed at the bottom of the email, and is a good option for genuine marketing emails that you do not want to receive, but not for fake ones.

> You are receiving travel offers for flights departing from as it is selected as your preferred country of departure. If you would like to change your country of departure or change the frequency of the emails you receive, you can modify your preferences. To stop receiving offers from Qatar Airways, click here to unsubscribe.

If you try to stop spam emails by replying or unsubscribing, the exact opposite will happen: by interacting with the email, this notifies the spammers that it is an active account and so they are likely to increase the volume of fake emails directed at the account. A better option is to keep sending fake emails to your Junk email account. After a period of time, the spammers (or the automated systems that create the spam) will realize that there is no reply from the account and move on to other options.

Fake Email Warnings

Varieties of fake emails are plentiful and potentially harmful, in that they could infect a computer with viruses, or con people to part with cash that they will never see again. There is also another form of fake email that does not have as damaging consequences, but can cause frustration to those who encounter it. This is a warning about a fake email that is in circulation, but the warning itself is inaccurate, as there is no fake email – it does not exist. This can cause the recipient to forward the email warning to all of their contacts, unaware that this is just creating unnecessary email traffic. If the recipients of the email do the same and forward it to their contacts, this causes a snowball effect of email warnings for a risk that is not there.

Fake email warnings are along the lines of:

"Hi Nick, I've just heard about the latest scam email that can freeze all your online accounts if you click on the link within it. It's called Freezer and seems to be spreading quickly. Could you email all your contacts to warn them about this?"

If you receive an email like this, the first thing to do is NOT forward it on to all of your contacts. Instead, do a search on the internet about the name used in the email, or the activity that it claims is done by the email. The chances are that other people will have come across this and so there will be information available about it, identifying it as a fake email warning. If the email is a genuine warning then this should be flagged up in an internet search too. There are also websites that specialize in publicizing email scams.

If you do receive a fake email warning from one of your contacts, the best course of action is to contact the person that has sent you the email. Let them know that you have checked about the contents of the email itself and identified it as a false warning. Hopefully, this will alert the sender of the original email and they will be able to prevent further distribution of the fake message by not sending it to any more of their contacts. If they have sent it to other contacts, they should then send a follow-up message explaining the situation.

Social Media Passwords

Using social media websites and apps can be a fun and productive way to keep in touch with family and friends. News and information can be posted to your social media account, and it can also be used to share a variety of information, including photos and videos. Once you have one social media account it is logical that you will want to add other sites to your online social media portfolio. There is no shortage of options, with sites including Facebook, Twitter, Instagram, and Snapchat all offering valuable online services for social media users.

However, as with other online accounts that you have, it is important to guard your social media accounts, so that no unauthorized people can gain access to them. The best way to do this is to use different passwords for each account. This may seem frustrating in terms of remembering different passwords, but if a criminal or a fraudster gets access to one of your social media passwords, they will have access to all of your accounts if they all use the same password. Use a password manager to create and store passwords for your social media accounts, and use the Remember Me option when you log in, so that the site remembers the password and you do not have to enter it each time that you log in to the site.

One of the fundamental functions of social media sites is to create links with your family and friends. For instance, you can add friends on Facebook, or choose to follow other people on Twitter. When you first start on a site such as Facebook, it is relatively easy to add friends: you search for your actual friends and, if they are also on Facebook, you can add them as a friend by sending them a request (as long as they accept it). Your friends can also send you a friend request, and this way you will be able to view items that they post on their pages and vice versa.

Once you are friends with someone on Facebook you will also have access to their friends, and you will receive Facebook suggestions for other people to befriend. This works well with family members and close friends, and it is a good way to add these people to your list of friends.

Although we all like to think we have a wide circle of friends, and would like our social media profiles to include as many friends or followers as possible, as a general rule, don't accept a friend request from someone you don't know and who isn't already a friend of one of your existing social media friends. Fraudsters and scammers operate within the social media world in the same way as in other online environments, with a view to conning money out of people or stealing their identity. Someone could create a false profile on a social media site, complete with photo and biographical details, and pretend to know one of your existing friends. If they become friends with you, they may then try to obtain sensitive information from you. Also, be very wary of accepting a second friend request from someone you are already friends with, as the second account could be a cloned account. These are common ways for criminals or fraudsters to befriend unsuspecting people online, sometimes with the promise of a romantic involvement. For children and teenagers, it is very important that they never arrange to meet a stranger who has befriended them on a social media site.

Although social media sites are ideal for sharing information with family and friends there are some areas that should be avoided, so as to not disclose too much information about yourself. If you do reveal sensitive information on your social media sites, it could be used by criminals or fraudsters to steal your identity. Some things that you should not publish on your social media websites include:

● Personal details such as your home address or phone number. These could be used by criminals to physically target your home, or send fraudulent messages to your phone via text messages.

● Details such as your mother's maiden name, as these could be used to impersonate you in online financial transactions that include security questions.

● If you are going on vacation, don't announce this on social media before you go: this is like giving criminals an open invitation to come and rob your home, since it is likely to be empty. Also, don't post vacation photos while you are away, as this is another sign that your home is empty. It may be difficult to resist, but wait until you get back home to show the world your vacation photos.

● Be careful of photos published on social media sites where sensitive information may inadvertently be in the background, such as a debit or credit card on a table behind you when you are taking a selfie. Information such as this can be used by fraudsters to try to access your bank account, and it can also be used as part of the jigsaw when identity fraud is being undertaken.

● Never publish anything inappropriate that could later be used against you. If you are in doubt about anything, then don't post it.

Unlike footprints in the sand, our online activity tends to leave a more permanent imprint, even if we think we have deleted something. Whatever we do online leaves a record, known as a digital footprint. Over time, this builds up until there is a vast amount of data about ourselves on the internet. Most of the time this is not an issue, but it is important to remember that something posted years ago on a social media site could still be accessed today. This could just be mildly embarrassing baby photos, but employers are increasingly looking at social media sites to see if there is anything incriminating about potential employees.

Digital footprints also apply to items that are published on social media sites in anger or in haste. Celebrities and politicians are frequently being caught out by social media posts containing inappropriate comments or language, even if the posts have been subsequently deleted. The problem with this is that digital footprints can easily be preserved: if there is a post on Facebook or Twitter, all it takes is for one person to take a screenshot of it for it to remain on the internet. The screenshot can then be published in its own right, thus causing the original publisher of the post even more embarrassment. The speed at which users can capture inappropriate posts should not be underestimated, and you should never presume that something has been permanently deleted from the internet.

On some social media sites it is possible to hide posts from certain groups of people, using specific privacy options. This can limit the audience for a post to your family and friends (or specific people), but if it is published on a social media site there is always the possibility that it can be distributed further afield, by other people.

Younger users of social media should be made fully aware of the potential permanence of their online activity and the potential it can have to affect them in later life. One good rule is to not publish anything about yourself that you would not like to see as the main headline in a newspaper.

Pause Before You Post

Social media is the symbol of the instant communication age that has been created by the internet. Since it creates the means to publish information at the tap of a button, many users feel that they have to respond immediately to every text, post, or tweet. There is even a perception that it is rude if a response is not given in a matter of minutes (or even, for some people, a matter of seconds). Although this can create an instantaneous flow of information, it can also have negative effects on users:

- People can become stressed if they feel they are not answering a message quickly enough: they feel pressure to show that they are part of the conversation. This can cause people to post messages to social media on their smartphones at times when it is not safe to do so: when driving, walking along the street, or even when riding a bicycle. (There have been cases where towns and cities have banned the use of smartphones when using street crossings, as it has caused too many accidents.) Always take a few moments to make sure that it is safe to use your mobile device in public to post something to social media. No message is so important that it is worth causing an accident.

- It is easy to become annoyed, or even enraged, by something that someone has published on social media. Everybody has an opinion, and social media has made it possible to get this message out to a global audience. If you see something on social media that makes you angry, resist the urge to post an immediate reply. Things said in haste or in anger are rarely productive and will probably result in an online argument, known as a "flame war". A much better approach is to take some time to consider a more measured reply or, in some cases, no reply at all may be best. Whatever you do post will not only be seen by the original poster, but also by all of your friends or even by the general public if you are replying to a post on a public page or group page. If you do have an issue with an online post, contact the person privately, through a private message or email.

Falling Foul of the Law

Despite how some people use it, content on social media is not above the law. Posting offensive material can cause a number of detrimental effects including:

- **Prosecution**. In some cases, offensive material can be subject to prosecution, including libel.

- **Banning from social media sites**. In extreme cases, users of social media sites will be banned because of the content that they publish. This is generally connected with areas such as promoting terrorism or hate speech.

- **Disciplinary action at work**. Many organizations will take disciplinary action against employees if they are deemed to be bringing the company into disrepute. This includes negative comments and activities on social media, even if they are not directly aimed at the company itself.

Some people use social media deliberately to be provocative or to further their own specific causes. Others publish items that are offensive or derogatory through poor judgment, rather than trying to support a specific agenda.

For any user of social media there should be some areas that are avoided, either on the grounds of taste, or because they may have legal consequences. These apply equally to individuals or groups and include:

- Hate speech.

- Racism.

- Bigotry.

- Sexual orientation.

- Misogyny.

It's Not All About You

By their nature, social media sites are designed to make a lot of information about people available online. However, before you start using social media it is important to be aware of the impact that your posts can have on your family and friends. Just as it is important to be careful about broadcasting your own personal information, it is equally important, or arguably more so, to be careful about what you publish about other people. Some areas to consider are:

- Do not publish any personal information about your family and friends, such as home addresses, phone numbers, or email addresses.

- Do not publish details about when family and friends are on vacation. Just as you do not want to alert criminals to the fact that your own home is empty, you also do not want to do it about people you know.

- If you are taking photos in the homes of family or friends, make sure that there is no sensitive information in the background.

- Do not post any gossip or unsubstantiated details about family members or friends. If you would not like to see the information posted about yourself then don't post it about someone else.

- If you are publishing photos that include other people's children, even if you are related to them, ask the parents or guardians for permission. Not everyone wants to have an online photographic record of their children, and you should be sensitive to these concerns.

- Be careful about wishing children of family members or friends a happy birthday on social media. Even the smallest piece of information can help fraudsters build up a profile of someone over time: they may not use it immediately, but it could be stored for use in the future, when more information has been gathered.

Beware of the Trolls

Trolls are the scourge of social media, and are a genuine problem in terms of polluting a powerful and effective communication tool. Sometimes known as "keyboard warriors" because they attack people from their keyboards with the anonymity of a nickname as their username, they post a torrent of spiteful and abusive messages, aimed at anyone whose views or opinions do not match their own. Trolls can have a significantly detrimental effect on the health and wellbeing of the recipient, and this can be particularly harmful to children and teenagers. Social media companies are taking active steps to try to diminish the impact of trolling, but it is a persistent and pervasive problem. However, there are some steps that can be taken to try to reduce the impact of trolling.

- Talk to children and teenagers and ask them if they have been subjected to trolling or online bullying. Actions that can be taken include contacting schools or local authorities, but make sure you do this with the consent and agreement of the person who is being targeted: if you take action against their wishes then you may make the situation worse.

- Report posts to the social media company. Most social media sites have a **Report** button that can be used to report offensive posts. This can start an investigative process against the person posting the offensive items.

- Report posts to the police. Trolls frequently publish direct threats to people, and in some cases this may necessitate police action. This should be considered if there is a credible threat to safety, but not for more minor issues such as someone criticizing the color of your shoes or your latest haircut.

- Block posts. As with reporting posts, most social media sites have an option to block comments from certain users appearing on your social media pages.

There are many exciting activities that can be undertaken on social media sites, but the most important one is when you have finished with a particular session: it is essential that you log out of the social media site. If you do not log out, anyone who has access to your device could use your social media account and post information pretending to be you. This could just be mischievous gossip, or fraudulent activities. This can cause considerable anxiety and disruption, particularly for younger users, so make it part of your routine to know where the log out button is, and always click or tap on it at the end of a session.

Some of the ways in which someone could impersonate you if you do not log out of your social media sites include:

- Posting items that are intended to be humorous but end up having potentially serious consequences. This can be particularly devastating for romantic relationships: if an imposter posts something negative about a partner, this could cause considerable problems before the correct person is able to rectify the situation.

- Offensive comments. Anyone who gains access to your social media account could post abusive or offensive comments that seem to be coming from you.

- Appeals for money. If someone has malicious intent and gains access to your social media account, they could use it for financial gain. If they have created a fake page for charity donations, they could post an item on your page, seeming to have come from you, detailing a charity appeal and including the link to the fake donations page. As your family and friends will believe the post has come from you, they may be more likely to donate on the fake page.

In addition to logging out of your social media site, make sure that your device is protected with a Lock screen password, so that it cannot be accessed in the first place.

Facebook is one of the most-used social media sites, and is ideal for connecting with family and friends and sharing news and other information. There is a huge wealth of data within Facebook, and there have been some security and privacy issues with the site in recent years. Although there have been steps taken to address these issues, it is impossible to give a 100% guarantee that your details on Facebook, and other social media sites, will not be made available to other people without your permission. It is therefore important to perform some security and privacy checks on your Facebook page. The first option can be to specify some security settings. To do this:

 Log in to your Facebook account and click or tap on the **Menu** button on the top toolbar

 Click or tap on the **Settings** button in the left-hand sidebar

3 The **Security** options are displayed on the Settings page. Click or tap on an option to view more details about it

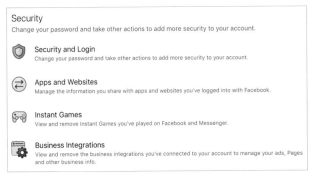

Security

Change your password and take other actions to add more security to your account.

🛡 Security and Login
Change your password and take other actions to add more security to your account.

🔁 Apps and Websites
Manage the information you share with apps and websites you've logged into with Facebook.

🎮 Instant Games
View and remove Instant Games you've played on Facebook and Messenger.

🏷 Business Integrations
View and remove the business integrations you've connected to your account to manage your ads, Pages and other business info.

Once Facebook security settings have been accessed as shown in Tip 61, it is possible to edit them in various ways. To do this:

Click or tap on a setting as shown in Step 3 of Tip 61

Click or tap on the **Edit** button next to one of the options

Apps and Websites

🔒 **Logged in with Facebook**   Edit >

These settings control the info you are sharing with other companies through apps and websites you've logged into using Facebook.

Preferences

⚙ **Apps, Websites and Games**   Edit >

This setting controls your ability to interact with apps, websites and games that can request info about you on Facebook.

Each option will have its own settings. For instance, with some you will be able to turn items **Off** so that they should not have access to your Facebook account and data

Platform

Apps, Websites and Games

This setting is **turned on**.

If you turn off this setting:

- You won't be able to log into apps or websites using Facebook
- Apps and websites you've logged into with Facebook may delete your accounts and activity
- You won't be able to play some games on Facebook, and your gaming activity may be deleted
- Your posts, photos and videos on Facebook that apps and websites have published may be deleted
- You won't be able to interact with or share content from other apps and websites on Facebook using social plugins such as the Share and Like buttons

Close	Turn Off

Facebook Privacy Options

In addition to security, another important issue for Facebook users is privacy. This relates to who can see what you post on Facebook and also how the data created by your account is used. To access the Facebook Privacy options:

 Log in to your Facebook account and click or tap on the **Menu** button on the top toolbar

Click or tap on the **Privacy Shortcuts** button in the left-hand sidebar

The options are displayed on the Privacy Shortcuts page. Scroll down the page to view the full range of available options

Privacy Shortcuts

Tools to help you control your privacy and security on Facebook

Privacy

Control who sees what you share on Facebook, and manage data that helps us personalize experiences.

Review a few important privacy settings

Learn about your privacy on Facebook

••• See more privacy settings

Although Facebook is great for sharing, many people do not want to share everything that they post with everyone who can view their account. To facilitate this, there is a privacy setting where you can select who can see your posts:

 Access the **Privacy Shortcuts** as shown in Tip 63. Click or tap on the **Review a few important privacy settings** in Step 3 in Tip 63

 In the **Privacy Checkup** window, click or tap on the **Next** button

Facebook

Let's start your Privacy Checkup.
Thanks for taking the time to do this. Now, let's go through 3 steps to help make sure you're sharing the info you want to share.

Next

 Click or tap in the **Choose Audience** box and select who you want to see your posts. This can include anyone (**Public**), but better options are **Family**, **Close Friends** or **Friends**

Posts
Whenever you post from News Feed or your profile, you can choose an audience to control who sees it.

Your next post

Choose Audience   ⚙ Custom ▾

Tip: You can change your audie

Next

● **Public**
Anyone on or off Facebook

👥 **Friends**
Your friends on Facebook

🔒 **Only me**
Only me

⚙ **Custom**   ✓
Friends

★ **Close Friends**
Close Friends

👤 **Family**
Family

Viewing Your Details

Within the Facebook privacy options it is also possible to view your Facebook information, including the activity that you have undertaken on your Facebook page. To view these details:

 Access the **Privacy Shortcuts** as shown in Tip 63. Scroll down the page to the **Your Facebook Information** section

Your Facebook Information
View or download your Facebook information at any time.

📇 Access your information

☰ See your Activity Log

📇 Manage your information

⬚ˣ Delete your account and information

 Click or tap on the **Access your information** option to view details of your Facebook activity. Click or tap on the arrow next to an item to view it

Your Information

Here is a list of your Facebook information that you can access at any time. We've categorized this information by type so you can easily find what you're looking for. Our Data Policy has more information about how we collect and use your information, how it's shared and how long we retain it. It also outlines your rights and how you can exercise them, and how we operate and transfer your information as part of our global services.

You can choose to download your information if you'd like a copy of it.

Your Information ℹ️

📄 **Posts**
Posts you've shared on Facebook and posts you've been tagged in ›

📷 **Photos and Videos**
Photos and videos you've shared or been tagged in ›

💬 **Comments**
Comments you've posted on your own posts, on other people's posts or in groups you belong to ›

Since social media sites are free to use, they have to generate their revenue somehow, and they do this through the use of advertisements. These appear on social media pages as users are entering posts and sharing information. On Facebook, ads are generally tailored to individual users, depending on their preferences and the types of content that they have looked at. However, there are some settings that can be applied in terms of how ads appear on Facebook pages. To do this:

 Access the **Privacy Shortcuts** as shown in Tip 63. Scroll down the page to the **Ad Preferences** section

 Click or tap on the **Learn about ads** option to see how Facebook uses ads on the site, and how they use your data in relation to them

Click or tap on the **Review your ad preferences** option in the previous step to see how Facebook uses your data in relation to the ads that you see. Click or tap on the **Your information** option to view how ads are displayed in relation to your

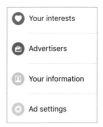

profile information. Click or tap on the **Ad settings** option to see how your data is used to display advertisements that are more specific to you, based on your profile. You can specify that you do not want ads to appear based on your profile, but this will not reduce the overall number

Social media companies are increasingly aware of the need to keep their users as safe as possible when they are on their sites. On Facebook there is an entire Safety Center that is dedicated to providing information about how users can make their online experience as safe as possible. To access it:

1 Access the **Privacy Shortcuts** as shown in Tip 63. Scroll down the page to the **Safety** section. Click or tap on the **Visit the Safety Center** option to view the Safety Center options

Safety
Learn about how we help you and your family stay safe when you use Facebook.

- Visit the Safety Center
- Find resources for parents
- Help prevent bullying

2 The Safety Center contains a range of information relating to online safety, privacy, and security. There are also portals for parents and young people, giving tips and advice about how to get the best and safest Facebook experience. Click or tap on one of the main headings in the left-hand panel to view all of the related information in the main window of the Safety Center

Account Security

In addition to the general security settings, Facebook also has a section specifically for account security, to ensure that your personal information and your login details are as secure as possible. To access these settings:

① Access the **Privacy Shortcuts** as shown in Tip 63. Scroll down the page to the **Account Security** section

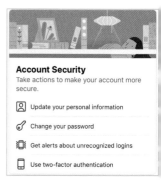

Account Security
Take actions to make your account more secure.

☐ Update your personal information

☐ Change your password

☐ Get alerts about unrecognized logins

☐ Use two-factor authentication

2 Click or tap on the options to **Update your personal information**, **Change your password**, or **Get alerts about unrecognized logins** to your account

 The final option is to **Use two-factor authentication** when logging in. This provides an extra level of security by requiring a code to log in, in addition to your username and password. The code can be sent to a mobile device or an app

Help Center

The Facebook Help Center is similar to the Safety Center in that it contains a wealth of useful information about using Facebook and solving potential problems. This should be your first port of call if you are unsure about how to do something on the site. To access the Help Center:

 Click or tap on the **Menu** button on the top toolbar, and click or tap on the **Help Center** button

 Use the Search box at the top of the window to ask questions relating to something you want to know about when using the Facebook site

 Click or tap on one of the buttons beneath the Search box to view details about specific topics

 Commonly asked questions are displayed beneath the buttons in Step 3. Click or tap on one to view the answer

Questions You May Have

↗ What names are allowed on Facebook?

↗ How do I choose what I get notifications about on Facebook?

↗ Where can I find my Facebook settings?

↗ How do I change or reset my Facebook password?

Regardless of whatever security measures are put in place for a Facebook account, there is still a chance that someone could hack into it and perform actions while pretending to be you. If you think this may have happened, due to any unusual activity within your account, or your Facebook friends alert you to any suspicious messages claiming to be from you, look in the Help Center for details about dealing with a hacked account:

 Access the Help Center as shown in Tip 69

 Enter **hacked account** into the Search box at the top of the Help Center

 Click or tap on one of the options relating to a hacked account. This depends on the activity that you think has been undertaken in your account. For each option there is a **Guided Help** option for taking you through the process of reporting the problem and restoring your account

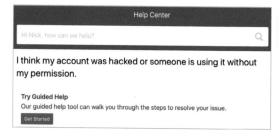

Deactivating an Account

Whenever you are finished with a Facebook session you should always log out, to avoid anyone else gaining access to your account. However, there may be times when you want to deactivate your account altogether, so people cannot see that you are available within Facebook. Accounts can also be deleted altogether but this is a more permanent and complicated process: if an account is deactivated, it can always be activated again by logging in to Facebook.
To deactivate your Facebook account:

 Access the **Privacy Shortcuts** as shown in Tip 63. Scroll down the page to the **Your Facebook Information** section. Click or tap on the **Delete your account and information** option

Your Facebook Information
View or download your Facebook information at any time.

- Access your information
- See your Activity Log
- Manage your information
- Delete your account and information

 Check On the **Deactivate Account** option and follow the wizard that takes you through the process. Once your account is deactivated, no-one will be able to view your Facebook page, and they will not see your name if they search for it. In effect, you are hidden from other Facebook users

Deactivation and Deletion

Deactivating or Deleting Your Facebook Account
If you want to take a break from Facebook, you can deactivate your account. If you want to permanently delete your Facebook account, let us know.

Deactivate Account
○ Deactivating your account can be temporary. Your profile will be disabled and your name and photos will be removed from most things you've shared. You'll be able to continue using Messenger.

Delete Account
○ Deleting your account is permanent. When you delete your Facebook account, you won't be able to retrieve the content or information you've shared on Facebook. Your Messenger and all of your Messages will also be deleted.

Continue to Account Deactivation

Identity fraud is the practice of using someone's name and personal details to perform criminal activity while pretending to be the person whose identity they have stolen. It is not confined to online activity, but the internet has undoubtedly made it easier for criminals and fraudsters to obtain individuals' personal details and then use them online for fraudulent purposes.

Identity fraudsters try to build up a profile of people over time, using a variety of personal information, including:

- Name and date of birth.

- Address.

- Mobile/cell phone number.

- National Insurance/Social Security number.

- Driver's license number.

- Utility bills information.

- Financial details such as online banking login details and PIN numbers.

- Credit card and bank card numbers.

- Online usernames and passwords.

Although certain pieces of information on their own may seem insignificant, such as your name, the more that the fraudsters can obtain, then the more convincing they can be when they pretend to be someone else. Identity fraud can be very distressing for its victims, and time-consuming and complicated to put right once it has been identified.

Once identity thieves have obtained enough personal information about someone, they can start performing activities while pretending to be that person.

Protecting Vital Information

Identity fraud can be a very distressing and expensive experience. It is therefore important to try to protect your personal information as carefully as possible, both in the real world and the virtual one. Some steps to take to do this are:

- Monitor bank and credit card statements to see if there are any suspicious or unexpected transactions. If there are, contact your bank or credit card provider immediately.

- Shred all paper documents containing personal information (see Tip 74).

- For online financial transactions, only use sites with a HTTPS at the beginning of the website address.

- Never respond to unsolicited requests for any of your personal information.

- Use anti-virus software and a firewall on your computer, to keep the information held on it as secure as possible, and always download the latest updates.

- Keep your digital devices locked with a secure password for the Lock screen.

- Use passwords that are as secure as possible – a minimum of eight characters with a mix of uppercase and lowercase letters, numbers, and symbols.

- Never using public Wi-Fi hotspots for conducting financial transactions with usernames and passwords.

- Ensure that old computing equipment that you dispose of has had all of the data wiped from its hard drive, or reset to its original state for a smartphone or tablet.

- Store any sensitive documents in a secure place, such as a home safe.

If important paper documents are thrown away they can be used by identify thieves to build up a profile of someone. Even something like a utility bill could be useful to fraudsters. Because of this, it is important to shred all potentially important documents before they are thrown away. The most secure way to do this is through the use of a micro-shredder: if a standard shredder is used, identity thieves can sometimes put documents back together and obtain important information from them. When looking at a micro-shedder some areas to consider are:

- How small does it shred the paper? The smaller the better, usually measured in millimeters or fractions of an inch.

- Use a shredder that operates horizontally and vertically (cross-shredding), rather than just in one direction.

- Use a shredder that can also shred plastic credit and bank cards.

One way to see if there has been any possible identity theft is to check your credit rating score. If you do this initially, you can then keep an eye on it to see if it changes drastically. If it does, this could be a sign that someone is undertaking financial transactions in your name, without your knowledge. Three credit rating websites to look at are:

- Experian

- Equifax

- TransUnion

For a monthly fee, these companies also offer more advanced identity theft protection.

Although the internet in general is a free resource, it supports the adage that, "you get nothing for nothing". Even when we are just browsing websites there can be a price to pay, in terms of individual sites tracking your activity and storing this data for future use. This could be related to the next time that you visit the site, and they may also make it available to third parties (although there are regulations intended to inform users how their data is used).

One way to check how websites are checking your browsing activity is to use a website tracker-blocking app. These can perform a number of useful tasks:

- Block advertisements on websites that track your activity (even if you do not click on them).

- Block invisible trackers that are designed to track your activity without your knowledge.

- Block trackers that claim to be on an acceptable list of advertisements, when they are not.

- Help websites load faster due to the number of website trackers that are blocked.

Browser settings for some browsers contain options for blocking website trackers, but a more comprehensive option is to use a dedicated tracker-blocking app that is designed specifically for this purpose. Some to look at include:

- Panopticlick

- Freedom

- RescueTime

Some website tracking blockers are free, while others charge a fee. Search the app store that is related to your device to find applicable website tracking blockers.

Reporting Identity Fraud

Identity fraud can be a traumatic experience, but to mitigate against its worst consequences it is vital that you take immediate action if you fear that you may have fallen victim to identity fraud. The longer you leave it, the more time that the criminals will have to perform transactions in your name. Also, you may be liable for some of the costs if you suspect identity theft but do nothing about it. There are several things that can be done if you suspect that you are a victim of identity fraud:

- Contact your bank and cancel all credit and bank cards. Inform the bank of the fact that you think you may be a victim of identity fraud so that they can freeze your accounts if necessary (you may need to make alternative arrangements for withdrawing funds until the identity fraud issue is resolved).

- Report any other lost or stolen documents to the issuing authority. This could include passport and driving license.

- Report the issue to your local police and make sure that you have a record of having made the report, in the form of a crime reference number.

- Report the issue to the national authority that is responsible for identity fraud. In the UK this is the CIFAS (Credit Industry Fraud Avoidance System), using their website at **cifas.org.uk**. In the US it is the Federal Trade Commission (FTC), using their website at **identitytheft.gov**. Each national authority will conduct further checks to ascertain the extent of the identity fraud. They will also be able to issue you with an identity theft report and a recovery plan.

Fast action is essential in limiting the damage of identity fraud and giving the authorities the best chance of catching the fraudsters. Do not delay if you suspect that you may be a victim of identity fraud.

While it is important to back up the digital data on your computer, laptop, tablet, and smartphone (see Tip 37), it is also important to keep copies of your hard copy documents, in case you are required to present them if you have been a victim of identity fraud (if the originals are stolen you will still have proof that they relate to you). Some of the items that you should keep copies of include:

- Passport.

- Driving license.

- National Insurance/Social Security Number.

- Utility bills.

- Bank statements.

- Credit card statements.

- Store card statements.

Due to the potentially sensitive nature of these documents it is important that they are stored in a safe and secure place. Ideally this should be somewhere other than your home, but if this is not possible, store them in a home safe (see Tip 79). One option is to arrange with a family member or friend to both use home safes and store each other's important documents in them.

Although creating and storing copies of your important documents can seem like a tedious chore, it is a lot more preferable to the alternative of identity fraud. To make the process more streamlined, create a schedule for when you copy and store important documents. For instance, this only has to be done once for a passport or driving license, but you may want to arrange to copy and store utility bills and bank statements every month, or quarterly.

Using a Home Safe

A home safe is a secure method of storage to give you
peace of mind about keeping your important documents in
your home. They are relatively inexpensive, with good quality
options starting from around £100/$100. Some of the
features to look for in a home safe include:

- **Digital keypad for opening the safe**. This should
  include options for a password of at least eight
  characters.

- **Key locking for opening the safe**. This should include
  at least two keys.

- **At least two locking bolts**. These are the bolts that
  physically lock the safe. More expensive versions usually
  have more bolts.

- **Fire resistant**. Some home safes have this as an option,
  in case of fire in the home.

- **Fixing for floor or wall**. There is little point in having
  a home safe if it could be just carried away from your
  home. Ensure it is possible to attach it securely to a
  wall or floor.

If you install a home safe it will not only be a means of
keeping your important documents secure, it could also
reduce your home insurance costs.

Online banking offers a range of benefits in terms of accessibility and ease of use: you can access your bank accounts and conduct a range of financial activities without even leaving your own home. However, as with all online activities that involve money, there are also a number of potential pitfalls.

Online banking can consist of two main elements:

- An online banking website where you can log in and access your account details.

- A companion banking app that uses the same login details as the online account. The app usually has a more limited range of services than the online version.

Each element of online banking can be used independently of the other (and only one is required to create an online account) but it is most effective to have an online account and the companion app. It is possible to create a new online bank account, or convert an existing one. Online accounts can still be managed physically through a branch office too.

When you first create an online bank account there are some security considerations:

- Use a strong password, of a minimum of eight characters, using uppercase and lowercase letters, and at least one number and one symbol.

- Some accounts also use a memorable word when logging in, in addition to a username and password.

- Never reveal your login details to anyone, even if they contact you claiming to be from the bank.

- Look for apps that use fingerprint ID or face ID for logging in to an account. This is more secure than only having a password.

Banking Security

It is important that you take your own security precautions when using online banking. In addition to this, examine the bank's website to see the security measures that they also put in place. Two areas to look for are:

- An online security guarantee or promise. This will give details about what the bank will do if there is fraudulent activity on your account (and it is not considered to be your fault; i.e., you have kept your security information safe and secure).

- A security center that contains details of actions that the bank takes to prevent online fraud. This should contain a range of information, including how to report any fraud you suspect. A link to a bank's security center should be displayed on its Homepage.

Potential Banking Scams

Banking scams are becoming increasingly sophisticated and will doubtlessly continue to do so, as criminals and fraudsters look for new and original ways to try to con people out of their money, using websites, email, and text messages to smartphones. Some of the existing online banking scams include:

- An email or text message claiming that there has been fraudulent activity on your account and that you need to transfer it to another account, mentioned in the message, to keep it secure. This simply gives the scammers access to your account, and a genuine bank would never ask you to do this.

- An email or text message claiming that there has been unusual activity on your account and asking you to click on a link in the message to confirm your password and security questions. Never click on a link in a message such as this, as it could give your login details to the scammers.

- An email or text message querying a card transaction that you have made and asking you to phone the number provided to check the transaction. Sometimes there is also an international number provided, but both are fraudulent. If in doubt, find a genuine number for your bank (e.g., from their website) and contact them using this to raise the issue.

- An email or text message saying that your account has been suspended and asking you to phone the number provided to verify your account details. A reputable bank would never ask for details in this way, and you should never disclose your full login details via text or phone, particularly when it is unsolicited.

- An email or text stating that you can view a credit card statement via the link in the message. A bank would never provide this type of message with a link.

Always Log Out

It is important to log out of any online accounts when you have finished using them, so that other people cannot gain access to them and perform actions in your name. With online banking this is doubly important, as it could lead to significant financial loss if someone else gains access to your online bank account when you have failed to log out and then left your device unattended. If this happens, you may also be liable for any financial losses, rather than being able to recoup them from the bank. Therefore it is important to follow two steps in relation to your online bank account:

- Always log out from an online banking session, on a website or when using an app. You may be asked to confirm that you want to log out: make sure that you click or tap on the **Log Out** button a second time if you are prompted in this way.

- Use the **Auto sign-out** option if the banking website or app has it. This means that you will automatically be logged out of your account after a specified period of inactivity. The shorter the length of time, the more security you have in case you forget to

Auto sign-out

Your security settings

To keep you secure, we'll automatically sign you out if you remain inactive for a given period of time or when you exit the app.

Sign me out:

Immediately after I exit the app ○

After one minute of inactivity ○

After two minutes of inactivity ◉

After five minutes of inactivity ○

After 10 minutes of inactivity ○

Save

log out. The auto sign-out option is usually found in the Settings section of the banking website or app.

Monitoring Your Accounts

It is important to be proactive when using online banking, so you can be the first person to spot any unusual activity. This includes checking your account and also being aware of some of the processes that are used when making transactions. Some areas to consider include:

- Always pause and take a moment to check any transactions that you have instigated yourself: double-check payment details to make sure that they are made to the correct person and account.

- If you receive any messages relating to your account, take some time to work out whether they are genuine or not. Do not click on any links or phone any numbers where your login details are required.

- Regularly check your online accounts (this is easy to do if you access them from your smartphone or tablet) to ensure there is no unusual activity.

- Use an online account that uses a One-Time Password (OTP) when you make a new money transfer or payment via your smartphone. This is a unique code that is sent to your smartphone that you can then use to verify the payment as being genuine.

- Verifying transactions. If you make a purchase for a larger sum than usual, your bank may contact you to verify the transaction. Although there are some fake messages that claim to be checking transactions, the genuine ones will not ask for any account details, but send you a text message asking you to verify whether certain transactions are genuine, using a Y for Yes or an N for No.

- If you have an online credit card, your bank should send you a message saying a statement is ready to view through your online banking site. The message may also include the last four numbers of the card.

Making Payments Online

One of the reasons for using online banking is to be able to make online payments. To do this, you need to have the recipient's name, bank account number, and bank sort code to identify the correct bank branch. When you enter these details, double-check them to make sure you are paying money to the correct account. There are also some security features that can be used to try to avoid payments to fraudsters. To make online payments:

Enter the payment details for the recipient. Select the **Pay later** option and select a specific date if you are unsure about a payee (this gives you the option of canceling the payment before the due date)

	Pay	
✕	To an external recipient	
From:	CURRENT ACCOUNT	>
To:		>
Amount:	£50.00	
Reference:	LUCY	
Date:		
○ Pay today	○ Pay later	
Payment purpose:		⌄

Select the type of payment. For some types, i.e., when paying for goods or services rather than to a family member, there may be a warning about the possibility of a fraudulent invoice or bank details

Paying for a service	⌄

If you've received an invoice or bank account details by email, this could be a scam.

What should I do?

Payment methods for goods and services evolve over time, with some methods diminishing in popularity over time. Methods that have been used include: cash, checks, and debit cards with PIN numbers. While these are still all in use to a greater and lesser extent, there is also a new method of payment available: contactless. This involves credit or debit bank cards being swiped over a card reader to make a payment, without the need for entering a PIN number. One of the other great advantages about contactless payment is that it can also be done with a smartphone. Making payments this way has two main advantages over using other forms of contactless payment:

- Contactless payment on a smartphone usually requires a fingerprint or face ID to confirm a payment, making it more secure than a card, which can be stolen and used without any additional

Face ID

security measures. Due to this, many countries do not have a limit for contactless payments with a smartphone, but they do for a credit or debit card.

- Although no form of contactless payment is 100% secure, using a smartphone is much safer, as no card information is passed between the retailer and the user: the transaction is done by sending an encrypted token that is used to authorize the payment. The token is stored on the smartphone, which indicates that the device has been authenticated for contactless payment.

Setting Up Contactless

Before contactless payment can be used on a smartphone it has to be set up on the device. The two main methods of contactless payment on smartphones are Apple Pay on the iPhone and Google Pay on Android smartphones. The process for setting up contactless payment is similar for both, and the example here is for the iPhone:

Open the app that is used to make contactless payments

Use the link to add a credit or debit card. This includes the account number and sort code of the issuing bank. These details can be entered manually, or the card can be scanned using the device's camera

Once the card details have been added, your bank or store card issuer has to verify your card. This can be done either by a text message or a phone call to your smartphone

Once the card's wizard is completed, details of the card appear in the app used in Step 1

To make a contactless payment with a smartphone, open the relevant app and tap on the card you want to use. Hold your smartphone up to the contactless payment card reader and use either fingerprint ID or face ID to make the payment

As well as using contactless payment on a smartphone in traditional bricks and mortar retail outlets, it is also possible to use it on websites and within apps that support this. Contactless payment can also be used within the related app stores for the smartphone. To use contactless payment on websites and within app stores:

- For online purchases on your smartphone, look for these symbols when you reach the checkout section of a website. Make the payment in the same way as doing it with a contactless payment reader.

- For app store purchases, confirm the payment with the same method as using a contact payment reader. In some cases, using contactless payment with the related app store has to be specified in the device's settings.

Investment Scams

A common type of financial scam is when fraudsters try to con people into paying money into fake investment opportunities. These take a number of forms, including:

- **Investments in fake companies**. These occur when the fraudsters send out communications via emails, text messages, and phone calls urging people to invest in a new, exciting company and large returns are promised on the investment. These are known as "boiler-room scams". However, the company, and the promised returns, do not exist. A search of the internet using the fake company's name should be enough to show that this is a scam. If you receive any kind of communication of this nature, ignore it: if you engage with the fraudsters they may use a degree of pressure to try to make you invest in their fake company.

- **Investments in cloned companies**. This is an example of when fraudsters create a website pretending to be an existing company. The website includes details about how people can invest in the company, and any investments go through the cloned website. There is usually a telephone number too, which is answered by someone pretending to be from the company who gives out investing details. When investing in shares of any company, do it through a recognized stock broker or online share dealing service rather than directly through a company's website.

- **Cryptocurrency**. The rise in popularity of cryptocurrencies (virtual currencies that are traded on the internet) such as Bitcoin has also seen an increase in fraud relating to them. The fraudsters create fake websites for trading cryptocurrencies and then persuade people to invest money via the website. After an initial investment, people are often encouraged to add more money to gain higher returns. When it is time to recoup the returns, the website is inactive and the fraudsters have long since disappeared.

For anyone who has responsibility for children, the internet can be fraught with worries and concerns. Many of these are well-founded, and you should take as many steps as possible to ensure that your child is as safe as possible when in an online environment. Some issues to consider include:

- Know how your child is accessing online content and, if possible, have them do this somewhere in the home where you are, so that it is not a secret.

- Talk to your child about the issues to do with online safety and also how they use the web. Create a partnership in terms of web use, and generate an atmosphere of trust with your child so that they can feel confident and secure when accessing content on the web. Using the web should be fun, and this involves both you and your child feeling secure and confident about their online activities.

- Encourage your child to tell you anything with which they are unhappy or unsure. Reassure them that they will not get into trouble for doing this, and that it is never wrong to flag up something they are concerned about. Openness is one of the best weapons against exploitation of children on websites.

- Try to avoid the temptation of checking up on your child by looking at their web browsing history. If they discover you doing this it may break any bond of trust that you have built up regarding their web use.

- Know how to report your own concerns. Either do this to the police, to your child's school, or through a national website that is dedicated to online protection and prevention of child exploitation. These websites contain details about how to make a report, and also a wealth of information relating to different age groups and the issues they could encounter on the web.

Social Media for Children

Safety on social media sites can be a major concern for parents and teachers. Talk to your child about this as much as possible, and be open with each other about your concerns and views. Some of the main issues are:

- Some sites have a minimum age limit for joining. However, there is no way for the site to enforce this, and so the only realistic way is through parental control. Despite this, it is still possible for children under the age limit to open an account at their friends' houses or other locations. Discuss this openly with your child and if you decide that you do not want them to have a social media account, explain your reasons.

- Even if you are friends with your child on a social media site such as Facebook, they will still be able to communicate with their peers via private messaging.

- Stress to children not to communicate with someone they don't know. People can set up fake accounts, so if they are contacted by someone they don't know, then ask them to report it to an adult or a teacher.

- Never let children advertise parties or social gatherings at your home through social media. A lot of small social gatherings have escalated into chaotic parties in this way.

- Nothing is private. Photos and comments can be copied and distributed to people via other means, such as email. Even private messages can be copied.

- Emphasize to children that even if they are annoyed with someone, don't post inappropriate comments about them. This can quickly get out of control and cause a lot of problems for all concerned.

- Stress that your child should never bully anyone on social media or post derogatory comments about them.

Some devices have a range of parental controls that can be deployed in relation to content being viewed on websites, or specific apps that are used. These controls are usually found within the device's settings, and some website browsers also have built-in options for parental controls.

As well as built-in parental controls, there is also a range of parental control apps that can be downloaded from a device's related app store. To do this:

1   Open the device's related app store and enter **parental controls** into the Search box

Review the result, and download the app that you want to use. Some parental control apps ask you to download a system profile for the app so that the controls can be communicated to the app's related website

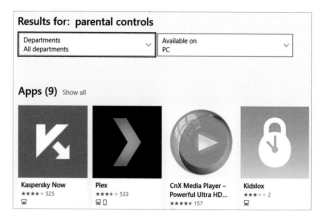

Results for: parental controls

Departments		Available on	
All departments	∨	PC	∨

Apps (9) Show all

Kaspersky Now	Plex	CnX Media Player – Powerful Ultra HD...	Kidslox
★★★★☆ 525	★★★★☆ 533	★★★★★ 157	★★★☆☆ 2

Open the downloaded app and create an account with an email address and a password to start setting parental controls for the device

When a child is using a digital device there are two options for controlling what they can, and cannot, do on it:

- Set it up as a child's device, and apply parental controls before they start using it, such as defining which apps they can use and the type of content they can access.

- Set it up as your own device, but use this device to control the device that a child is using.

If you are using a parental controls app, you can specify whether the device is your own or a child's when you start using the app. The subsequent options will differ depending on what is selected at this point.

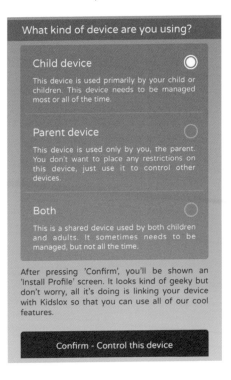

The issue of children viewing inappropriate content on websites or via apps and games is one of the biggest concerns for parents or guardians. However, through the use of parental controls apps, and also specific settings within a computer's operating system, it is possible to restrict the type of content that a child can view:

● From the **Accounts** setting in Windows 10, family controls can be accessed for a specific user. Within this it is possible to block inappropriate content from websites, apps, games and media.

● In parental controls apps, types of content, and specific apps, can be blocked by selecting the item so that it shows a locked padlock next to it. If there is an open padlock this means that the item can be accessed.

Setting Age Restrictions

Another area for applying online restrictions relates to age-appropriate content: if a 10-year-old is using a digital device it will not be appropriate for them to view content that is rated for 15-year-olds and above. Age restrictions can be set by specifying the age of the child that is using the device:

 Within a parental controls app, or the family controls option from the Accounts setting on a Windows 10 PC or laptop, select the age of the person using the device

> Allow apps and games rated for
>
> Any age (no restrictions) ⌄
>
> 13-year-olds
>
> **14-year-olds**
>
> 15-year-olds
>
> 16-year-olds

2 Once the age has been determined, select the ratings options to view the type of age-related content that can be viewed by a user of that age

> Allow apps and games rated for
>
> 14-year-olds ⌄
>
> View allowed ratings

×

Allowed content ratings

These are the standard content ratings for the age limit you set for your child.

12	Apps	For ages 12 and over
12	TV	For ages 12 and over
🎬	Films	For ages 12 and over
12	Music	For ages 12 and over
🎮	Games	For ages 12 and over

Setting Time Restrictions

Restricting the amount of time that children spend using digital devices is another function of parental controls apps. There are two options for this:

- Set a daily time limit for the maximum amount of time that the device can be used. Different times can be set for different days, and the limit for each day can be edited by selecting the day.

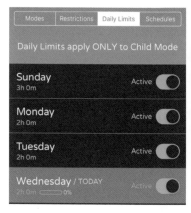

- Specify a schedule during which times the device cannot be used; e.g., for bedtimes. As with overall time limits, the schedule can be applied to individual days so that, for instance, a different schedule can be created for weekdays and weekends.

Setting Up Screen Time

To try to cut down the amount of time that people spend on digital devices, smartphones and tablets are increasingly using a function to monitor the amount of screen time that you use; i.e., how long you spend looking at your smartphone or tablet during the day. A report is generated that shows how long you have been using the device for, and the apps that you have accessed the most. Some devices can use apps to track your screen time, and there is also a built-in function for this on the iPhone and iPad. To set this up:

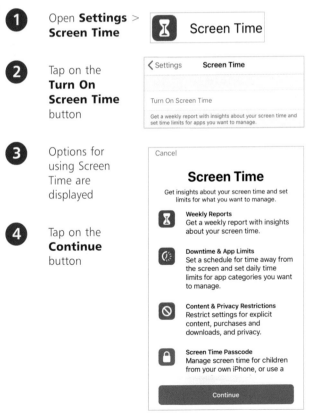

1. Open **Settings** > **Screen Time**

   ⧖ Screen Time

2. Tap on the **Turn On Screen Time** button

   ‹ Settings   **Screen Time**

   Turn On Screen Time

   Get a weekly report with insights about your screen time and set time limits for apps you want to manage.

3. Options for using Screen Time are displayed

4. Tap on the **Continue** button

   Cancel

   # Screen Time

   Get insights about your screen time and set limits for what you want to manage.

   ⧖ **Weekly Reports**
   Get a weekly report with insights about your screen time.

   ⧗ **Downtime & App Limits**
   Set a schedule for time away from the screen and set daily time limits for app categories you want to manage.

   🚫 **Content & Privacy Restrictions**
   Restrict settings for explicit content, purchases and downloads, and privacy.

   🔒 **Screen Time Passcode**
   Manage screen time for children from your own iPhone, or use a

   Continue

Once Screen Time has been activated, it can be used to monitor your screen and app usage:

 The current usage is shown at the top of the Screen Time window. This will be updated throughout the day

 The options for Screen Time include **Downtime**, **App Limits**, **Always Allowed** and **Content & Privacy Restrictions** (see Tip 99)

‹ Settings	**Screen Time**	
SCREEN TIME		Today at 13:14
Nick's iPhone		›

13m

Reading & Reference	Entertainment	Productivity
6m	50s	46s

Downtime
Schedule time away from the screen. ›

App Limits
Set time limits for apps. ›

Always Allowed
Choose apps you want at all times. ›

Content & Privacy Restrictions
Block inappropriate content. ›

Use Screen Time Passcode

Use a passcode to secure Screen Time settings, and to allow for more time when limits expire.

Share Across Devices

You can enable this on any device signed in to iCloud to report your combined screen time.

Turn Off Screen Time

 Tap on the **Use Screen Time Passcode** option to set a passcode that has to be entered to override any of the restrictions that have been applied within Screen Time; i.e., when a specific limit has been reached

Screen Time Options

To use the Screen Time options in Step 2 of Tip 98:

Tap on the **Downtime** button to access options for when the device cannot be used. Within the **Downtime** section, tap on the **Start** and **End** buttons to select times for when only specified apps are available

> **Downtime**
> 22:00 - 07:00

Tap on the **App Limits** button and then tap on the **Add Limit** button to add time limits for using types of apps

> **App Limits**
> Set time limits for apps.

Tap on the **Always Allowed** button. The apps that are always allowed to operate, regardless of what settings there are for Screen Time, are displayed. Tap on the red circle next to one to remove it. Tap on the **Choose Apps** button to add more apps that are allowed

> **Always Allowed**
> Choose apps you want at all times.

Tap on the **Content & Privacy Restrictions** button and drag the Content & Privacy Restrictions button to **On** to apply restrictions for blocking inappropriate content

> **Content & Privacy Restrictions**
> Block inappropriate content.

The Screen Time options can be used to apply specific settings for a child, so that you can have a degree of control over what they are using. These are similar to the standard Screen Time options, but they can be set up with an initial selection of wizards, and it is also possible to include a parental passcode that has to be entered when limits are reached. To set up restrictions for children:

 Access Screen Time options as shown in Tip 97 and tap on the **This is My Child's iPhone** button

‹ Back

Is This iPhone for Yourself or Your Child?

Screen time for a child's iPhone lets you set up additional parental controls.

This is My iPhone

This is My Child's iPhone

2 Select options for **Downtime**, **App Limits**, **Always Allowed** and **Content & Privacy Restrictions** and apply restrictions as required, such as the times the device can be used

Downtime

Set a schedule for time away from the screen. Your permission will be required to allow more screen time. Calls, messages, and other apps you want to allow can still be used.

Start   22:00

End   07:00

Set Downtime

Not Now

Access the **Use Screen Time Passcode** option as shown in Step 3 in Tip 98 and enter a passcode that has to be entered to override any of the restrictions for your child's device

Parent Passcode

Create a passcode that will be required to allow for more time, or to make changes to Screen Time settings.

○ ○ ○ ○

1	2 ABC	3 DEF
4 GHI	5 JKL	6 MNO
7 PQRS	8 TUV	9 WXYZ
	0	⊗

Notes

Notes

Notes

Notes